War & the Soldiers of Rome

War & the Soldiers of Rome

Uniforms, Weapons, Fortifications,
Structure and Tactics

ILLUSTRATED WITH 109 PICTURES,
PHOTOGRAPHS & DIAGRAMS

The Roman Soldier
Amédée Forestier

The Roman Soldier at War
H. Stuart Jones

LEONAUR

War & the Soldiers of Rome
Uniforms, Weapons, Fortifications, Structure and Tactics
ILLUSTRATED WITH 109 PICTURES, PHOTOGRAPHS & DIAGRAMS
The Roman Soldier
by Amédée Forestier
The Roman Soldier at War
by H. Stuart Jones

FIRST EDITION

Leonaur is an imprint of Oakpast Ltd
Copyright in this form © 2019 Oakpast Ltd

ISBN: 978-1-78282-834-1 (hardcover)
ISBN: 978-1-78282-835-8 (softcover)

http://www.leonaur.com

Publisher's Notes

The views expressed in this book are not necessarily
those of the publisher.

Contents

The Roman Soldier

IMPERATOR

Originally, as here, the victorious Roman general, saluted with this title by his soldiers in the field. The Emperors, however, usurped the title exclusively for themselves as a matter of hereditary right.

Contents

THE
ROMAN SOLDIER

SOME ILLUSTRATIONS REPRESENTATIVE OF
ROMAN MILITARY LIFE
WITH SPECIAL REFERENCE TO BRITAIN

BY

AMÉDÉE FORESTIER

WITH AN INTRODUCTION BY
IAN A. RICHMOND, M.A.
Department of Archæology, Queen's University, Belfast

A. & C. BLACK, LTD.
4, 5 & 6 SOHO SQUARE, LONDON, W.1
1928

Introduction

The Roman world in general, and Roman Britain in particular, have been of recent years much in the public eye. Newspapers have boomed them: schoolmasters have praised them: and an increasing number of wise visitors have learnt what a pleasant holiday can be spent among the Roman monuments of our island, from the south coast, with its great fortresses like Pevensey and Porchester, to the valleys of the Tyne and Irthing, where Hadrian's frontier-wall graces its lofty pedestal of basalt crags. Such visitors are not deep students. They journey to see historical remains in the spirit of Canterbury pilgrims; yet they are not undesirous of understanding what they see. But the game of holiday-learning has conditions; the facts presented should be entertaining and simple, rather than tame and complicated. So, it is that in historical guiding, local *ciceroni,* who know the rules, win more points than those who do not.

Accordingly, specialists will find in this hook only the simple facts which they have assimilated long ago. It is meant to supply pilgrims to our Roman monuments with statements which neither local guides nor antiquaries tend to give them Mr. Forestier offers here in picture, simple answers to those first questionings about the Roman Army which occur to anyone considering Roman history for the first time. What manner of men were the Roman soldiers? How did they come to dominate, by gradual process, Italy, the Mediterranean Basin, and Western Europe, not to mention Palestine, the Balkans and Asia Minor? Had they some special gift for fighting: or was their equipment better than that of their opponents? How did it happen that many soldiers of the Empire were not natives of Italy? Why did Mr. Kipling eventually give us the masterly picture of Britons fighting Rome's battles in their own country? Or how came Kingsley to write his lurid description of Gothic free-lances upsetting the high life of Alexandria, the greatest City of Roman Egypt?

Like all soldiers of the ancient world, the Roman soldier was originally the able-bodied man of a small community, fighting to protect his folk and his lands from jealous neighbours. There can be no doubt that the Romans were right in believing that they themselves became such soldiers as soon as Rome existed: so we go back to the middle of the eighth century before Christ, when the city had been founded upon a group of hillocks in the lower Tiber valley, where was a good river-crossing and fertile soil, exciting the jealousy of the hill-folk nearby. The organisation of this first army is obscure, but analogy and tradition combine to show that, in order not to disturb the balance of power within the State, it was levied from the noble caste, and commanded by the king. The armour worn, as remains of burials show, did not differ much throughout Italy. But types were not yet classified, and much experiment was in progress. Offensive weapons were still the cutting-sword, carried upon the shoulder-strap, and the long thrusting-spear, both adapted to stand-up fighting at close quarters. It was necessary to make a stand in order to defend fields as well as hearths, since the loss of crops might have grave consequences for a small and isolated community.

North of the Alps, where life was less settled, and in Greece, where land-hunger induced war, necessity compelled invention to march rather faster than in Italy. But even so early as the eighth century, the Etruscans (roving folk from the Near East, as is now universally understood) were bringing with them to Italy armour of essentially Greek type. Owing to its cost and cumbrousness, this armour never completely ousted the lighter and more pliant Italic type. Yet it created a standard of heavy-armoured infantry which was to last for some time.

It quickly became clear, however, that if good armour was the deciding factor in pitched battles, wealth was as important as nobility. This determines the next stage. The Roman state and her rivals grow, and the new model army, introduced by King Servius Tullius in 578-535 B.C., so tradition has decided, is based entirely upon quotas of wealth. All property-owning citizens serve as soldiers, and are arranged according to wealth and age. The regulation armour is graded by wealth, and the heaviest armed receive smiths for field-repairs. Discipline, the *stabilimentum Romani imperii,* is already recognised as sufficiently important to demand the institution of special divisions of buglers and trumpeters, who play tunes appropriate to special needs. Cavalry is organised; the horses and fodder are provided by a special tax, paid by widows and orphans who cannot fight. The arrangement of this army in battle has been much discussed. But it is clear that, whatever the details, the whole scheme is a close battle-line, six deep, based upon a stationary conception of fighting, and unsuited to quick movement or extended order. The army is still organised for home service.

Tradition dates the first important adaptation to the needs of foreign service to the time of the war against the neighbouring town of Veii. The campaign involved a ten-year siege (406-396), and the Roman soldier both went into winter-quarters and received pay for the first time. He is not yet a professional; but pay is required in order to compensate for so long an absence from home. The need for frequent aggressive warfare introduces a more open battle order; and a new weapon is invented, the heavy javelin *(pilum,)*, which is thrown before charging, and has a soft point, meant to bend and stick in whatever it penetrates. This is to be of great help in crippling those who depend for defence upon the shield.

Much attention also is being paid to the art of encamping for the night. Soldiers are expected to be able to entrench themselves behind a mound and portable stakes, and their disposition in camp assumes regular order. In high command, the place of the king is now taken by one or both of two consuls. elected yearly, and not always fitted to command armies. But this disadvantage is for the moment glozed over by the discipline and orderliness of the army, unequalled inside or outside of Italy. The Roman *burghers* have become the *Stosstruppen* of their day.

The orderliness thus acquired is accompanied by a standardisation in armour. A metal-plated leather cuirass is evolved and worn by those who have the property-qualification to warrant the expense, while the poorer soldier wears a square breast-plate. And there is invented a new kind of shield, oblong in shape and convex: it is four feet high, and can be used to form a wall against charges, or a roof against missiles. Blows glance off the convex surface. So, the army is now equipped for the offensive; and by the formation of alliances, by their breakdown, and by the formation of counter-alliances in turn, the Roman soldier comes to be acting throughout Italy.

The allied states are expected to provide contingents for the army; but these are inferior in numbers. efficiency and discipline. Usually they provide light-armed troops and cavalry, in which the Roman Army is deficient. The new army is almost universally successful, if well commanded, but it is not exempt from disaster amid new experiences. By a great charge with their sweeping swords. the Gauls mowed the Roman line down at the Allia (390), while Pyrrhus was to win later (280) a great victory by means of an elephant charge at Heraclea. But neither defeat was decisive; and the Romans soon learnt to adapt themselves to the new ways of fighting. The fault was more often with the consul commander than with the soldier.

The Change from Local to Imperial Needs

Until the close of the second century B.C., the army remains much the same. But it has become much more expert. It has had to face the long Hannibalic Wars, during which the whole freedom of Italy was at stake. And its success there is due to patience and discipline much more than to brilliant tactics. Many times, the inefficiency of a consul almost lost all. Even discipline, which some commanders make a fetish, is grossly neglected by others, with disastrous consequences. On the whole, the army is becoming much more technical.

The construction of spring-guns and siege-machinery comes to be studied as an art; the erection of an encampment is a matter of rule, and Polybius gives us a glimpse of the soldier-surveyors with their different coloured ranging-flags. But the war is an immense strain. After a great disaster like Cannae (216) slaves and ex-slaves have to be enrolled in the army. Still greater is the strain on the Italian allies, who are now becoming subjects rather than equals. The aid of mercenary troops from allied sovereigns or states outside Italy is not disdained, and this marks the beginning of an important method of supplementing the Burgher Army. In Rome itself recruiting becomes detested and evaded.

Despite the grievous lack of professionalism and coordination, the system survived the Punic wars. But soon afterwards, when it became necessary to govern already Spain, Macedonia, Greece, Tunisia, and presently, the South of France and Illyria, the collapse began. In order to govern these provinces, the yearly magistrates, consuls and *praetors*, received provincial governorships as extensions of their year of office. This system relied too much upon the personal quality of the governor; and the police-work and guerilla warfare in the provinces and on the frontiers is wearing out the Burgher Army. Yet it is surprising what can be done. Already by 133, the armies before Numantia are constructing field-works equal in size and technical excellence to much of the work done by professional armies in later days.

Important buildings, like granaries and barracks, have already arrived at something like standard pattern. No other army in the world is capable of constructing such field-works. But decay is setting in rapidly. By the end of the second century the citizen cavalry is gone, and in its place are enrolled auxiliary levies from the tribes of Gaul, Numidia, or Spain. The discontent in Italy is reaching fever-pitch. The principle that legionaries must be men of property still exists; the Romans are doing all possible to evade service; and more work is being foisted upon the unhappy Italian allies.

Nor is the heavy infantry adapted to guerilla warfare; it has borrowed the Iberian stabbing-sword, but has not yet learnt to use it. Only towards the end of the century is the principle of drill borrowed from gladiators and introduced by Rutilius in Gaul, in order to enable the soldier to stand against mighty Gallic swordsmen. But the innovation came too late to save the Burgher Army. At the close of the century, during the African war and the Cimbric invasions of Italy, thousands of citizens became martyrs to inefficiency, and demonstrated that the old-world conception of the army was impracticable.

It fell to Marius, once a private soldier, to introduce the needed reform. The property-qualification for the legionary was abolished, and thus the character of the army was completely changed, for it could be adopted as a profession by the poor citizen. But this introduced a terrible danger to the state. The army now consisted of soldiers of fortune; and provincial governors, whose status has been noted, or generals, could now receive extensions of command to finish a given war. Suppose such a proconsul raised a faithful army, attached to him personally, who could turn him out of his command? Might he not become Dictator? This temptation to absolutism was great. It ruined Marius; it created Sulla. Presently, Crassus, Pompey and Caesar were all to play for the same stake. Antony and Augustus repeated the process, and the end of it all was the Julio-Claudian Imperial House. In sixty years, the reforms of Marius killed the Republic.

Yet these reforms were just in time to title the state over an unbelievably grave crisis. The allies, unable to hear their woes any longer, engineer a great revolt. Rome is to be wiped out, and the new army is strained to the utmost in quelling the attempt. The principle of levying provincial troops *en masse,* and of giving to them the citizenship at discharge for services rendered, is recognised for the first time; and these non-Italic citizens, and their sons (Spaniards in the known case), become eligible for service in the legions. After the revolt there is an equally important change. All Italy to the Po (and soon to the

Alps) receives the citizenship, and so the burden of legionary service is extended from the Romans to Italians the world over. There are no more Italian "allies," and the tendency to enrol and enfranchise provincials continues. The stage is set for personalities who will gather about themselves a force to master the state. And the soldier remains Roman, but Roman in quite a new sense.

THE IMPERIAL ARMY

During the last century of the Republic all the tendencies so far described come to a head. For a moment, after Sulla had placed the machinery for controlling the appointments to provincial governorships in the hands of the Senate, it looked as if the constitution so reformed was going to be strong enough to save itself from *pronunciamenti* or military conspiracies. But by giving to Pompey the command of the whole Mediterranean for a Pirate War, the Senate committed political suicide. Henceforward the whole aim of every notable politician was to create such a command for himself. When Caesar has built up a great army in Gaul, the time is ripe for the dissolution of the Republic; and the main question becomes whether anyone strong enough to control the armed forces will arise, or whether the whole Roman world will disrupt amid internal conflict. After the fall of Caesar, the position becomes so bad, that there is danger of the establishment of a monarchy on Eastern lines.

In the end Augustus emerges triumphant; and by slow stages he reforms the constitution, holding old Republican offices in new fashion and combination, and graced by the old title given by soldiers to their victorious general, Imperator. The government of military provinces is left in his hands, and administered through his legates, commanding limited troops through subordinate legionary legates, in turn appointed by the Emperor. The number of standing legions, each 4,000–6,000 strong, is settled for each province. Definite quarters are built for them; they become ultra-professional and steadily more provincial. Standing-quarters create small towns, in which a traditional soldier-class is reared. Some legions at first share quarters; but this. is too dangerous. It may cause grave mutinies, as in Pannonia. Again, the command of one or two legions among so few makes *pronunciamenti* possible.

After the close of Nero's reign there is an epidemic of them, not entirely stamped out until the end of the century. Joint encampments are abolished by then. But with the danger-limit of legions so low, the problem of Imperial Defence becomes complicated. Slowly the conquests of Caesar in north-western Europe are rounded off. Early in the first century an Elbe-Danube frontier becomes a brief possibility; then the line recedes to the Rhine, and bulges out again to the Neckar. Britain is taken over, though the conquest is never completed; and early in the second century, Dacia and Arabia are added by Trajan. Citizen-legions cannot garrison effectively all those provinces, and, in order to solve the problem, the old auxiliary system is developed upon a large scale.

Corps of provincials are levied from suitable peoples, and are quartered—five hundred or a thousand in paper strength—in forts of standard type, linked by military roads, which form lines of penetration or networks all over the frontier lands, and radiate from legionary fortresses. These folk use their native arms and make good frontier troops, half-soldier, half-police, receiving the citizenship on discharge after twenty-five years' service. The frontiers become so settled that it is possible to control and watch all slight movements upon them, and to extract valuable dues at the entrances to the Empire. Much thought and energy is spent upon perfecting frontier control: frontier-roads receive block-houses and signal-stations. Boundaries are marked and become barriers: they are supplied with forts and a large garrison of auxiliaries. The barriers assume definite military form, and soon Hadrian's Wall will provide a classic example of such evolution.

Normally the system works perfectly, and in the second century it is the regular mode of frontier control all over the Empire. But it is not designed against invasions. In those moments the legions emerge and are expected to deal with the trouble. When they do not, there is a big disaster. But the frontier land is usually a wide net, in which the invaders can be caught without disturbing the peaceful non-military world. In times of peace the soldiers are kept busy with useful tasks of construction, not only in the military area, but outside it. Road-systems, dykes or canals, aqueducts or bridges, and frontier works are thus constructed without great expense. The soldiers build their own forts and quarters: But the work is usually done by legionaries who are more intensively trained, and have richer traditions than the auxiliaries.

During the second century, however, the sharper of these distinctions are passing away, as once the distinction between Roman and Italian had done in Italy. As more provincials receive the citizenship, and as the legionaries, often themselves provincial, marry provincial wives, the sympathy of the army becomes steadily more provincial and less Italian.

At the end of the century the feeling is so strong that Severus can enrol in the Imperial Guard legionaries who horrify the Capital by their bearing and uncouth language. The legionaries are now recruited on the spot, and are permitted by Severus to live out of barracks with their wives. The principle of local recruiting also applies to auxiliary regiments. Whatever their original nationality, they now absorb the natives of the province wherein they are located; and recruits all become citizens on their discharge, and they or their sons are eligible for the legions. In the end the legions become the Senior Service, and there is little real difference between them and the auxiliaries except in weapons, drill and name. The fact is recognised by Caracalla, who extends in 214 the citizenship to all free-born in the Empire. Within the Empire there is now no bar to service in the legions whatever. From becoming Italian, with provincial auxiliaries, the army has now become entirely provincial.

This system has grave dangers which emerge in the third century. The provincial spirit in the army now fosters the first-century idea that Emperors need not be set up from Rome as a matter of course. It finds expression the moment that the supply of good Emperors fails. Commodus is followed by generals like Albinus of Britain, Pescennius Niger, and Sever us. Forty years later *pronunciamenti* have become chronic, and it looks as if the time of Rome's power were fulfilled. External troubles arise amid disaster within the Empire. The frontiers are robbed of troops: and the temptation to raid is too great for the jealous non-Roman world. By 275 the neglect has lost for ever both Dacia and the Neckar line.

But recovery is still possible. Provincialism has not yet bred nationalism. The Gallic National Empire is a great failure, and raises no spirit contrary to Latin civilisation. In the end there is only one solution. The big provinces, all Imperial by now, and the legions must be divided, while bureaucracy multiplies. When order is restored, the whole system is reformed thoroughly by Diocletian, and Constantine continues his work. Reduced to one thousand strong, the legions are redistributed all over the Empire, though some portion of the old unit is usually retained in its old quarters. The frontier garrisons are left where they are; but they are legally tied to the spot, and not allowed to desert the service. Frontier guard-duty becomes a hereditary trade.

A principle begun in the second century comes into wide use in the fourth, and the frontier corps are supplemented by new drafts of unfixed number, enrolled *en masse* from tribes outside the Empire. So, in its last brilliance the Empire revives the old solution of the moribund Republic. These barbarian troops, mixed with drafts from the legions, come to form an Imperial field force. But how long will the Empire stand the strain? It has to assimilate these foreign elements and make them good and loyal citizens. Again, by the end of the century, all the high army commands are passing to Teutons, and Teuton troops make up the army list of Honorius on an alarming scale. Half is provincial, and half utterly non-Latin and barbaric. Nor is the outside world slow to perceive this change. Between the quarrels of the Imperial House, the treachery of provincial governors, and the eager press of external nations to enter the lucrative and gorgeous Imperial Service, the Empire is reeling.

By the opening of the fifth century an external king like Alaric is asking for a share in the Empire, and receives the dignity of Master of the Horse, vindicating his claim by taking Rome. Stilicho, himself a Vandal, is not exempt from suspicion of collusion. Only a push is needed, and the whole top-heavy structure will fall. Presently the long-expected disaster comes—the great wave of Huns, the worst invasion Europe has had to face for centuries, sweeps into the west. It is broken at Châlons, by the united Roman and Visigothic armies. But the recoil is as disastrous as the blow; it disturbs all Central Europe, already in a ferment, and the West-Roman Empire comes to an end amid a welter of folk-wanderings.

Ian A. Richmond

Illustrations and Descriptive Notes

PRIMITIVE BRONZE-AGE WARRIORS

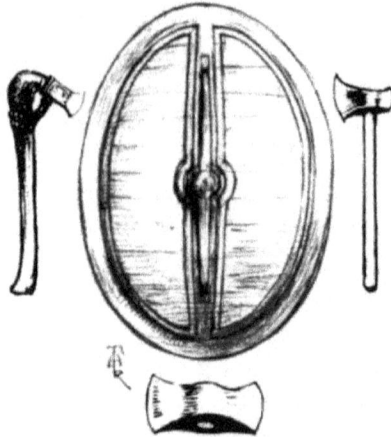

Weapons ill-adapted for skilful fighting:
wooden shield (*scutum*), with bronze boss
(*umbo*) and brace (*spina*) for reinforce-
ment; axes badly hafted, with small blades.

IN FACING DIFFERENT CLIMATES AND CONDITIONS

BRONZE-AGE WARRIORS. To the right is a
brazen-armed Greek, who protects his
cramped territory by a standing fight in the
heat. Hence the difference in costume.
Northerners struggle for existence in cold
climes, but less restricted space.

The figure on the left represents a Gaulish
chief, reconstructed by the Abbé Bourgeois
from discoveries at Hautcrive. He wears
a conical helmet and a short sword with
small hilt. Seated is a Gaulish chief of the
Danubian region; he has a double-crested
globular helmet, and a tall sword with a
peculiar hilt of bronze and iron.

22

BRONZE-AGE WARRIORS 800 B.C.

Swords and daggers: a stage in evolution
which did not last; the sword is too short
to slash, the dagger too long to stab. (*a*)
and (*b*) are bronze swords used by the first
Romans; (*c*) a dagger with triangular
blade; (*d*) a short sword (*gladius*) of
bronze and iron.

ITALY ADAPTS THE NORTHERN TYPE TO HEAT

ITALIC BRONZE-AGE SOLDIERS ON LOOK-OUT.
About 1000 B.C. The cuirasse and helmet
are still primitive, Greek improvements
have not yet arrived.
The standing figure has a spear with a
bronze head, a two-piece helmet and decorated pectoral. His oval shield is of
wood. The helmet of the kneeling figure
is round, with pointed top; he carries the
circular shield (*clipeus*).

ITALIC BRONZE-AGE WARRIORS ON LOOK-OUT

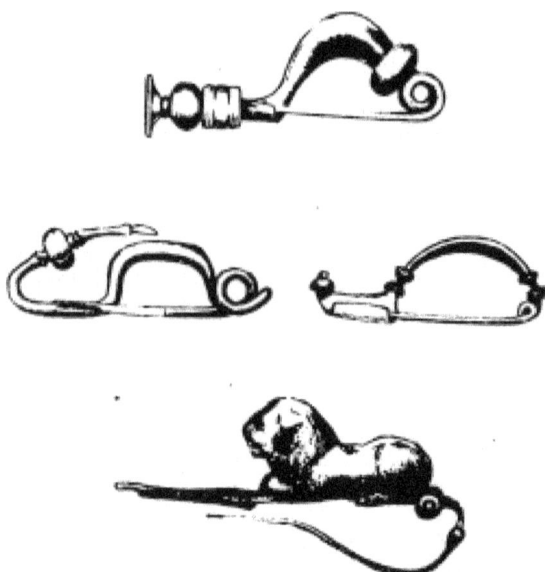

Cloak-pins (*fibulæ*), required for heavy
material, give scope for rich ornamentation
in gold, silver and bronze.

PRESENTLY THE HIGH STANDARD OF THE BRONZE-AGE

AN ITALIC FARMER OF THE BRONZE-AGE
ARMING FOR BATTLE. The typical bronze-
age equipment descends to the middle and
lower classes. The farmer wears a bell-
shaped bronze helmet strapped under the
chin. His round shield is painted or em-
bossed, sometimes with protective charms.
His javelin has a long narrow quadrangular
head.

An Italic farmer of the Bronze-Age arming for battle

A primitive helmet of the bronze-age, from a specimen found in a grave on the Esquiline at Rome. The chin-strap is of leather.

578 B.C.-538 B.C.

BECOMES THE LOW STANDARD OF THE NEXT

A HOPLITE IN THE ARMY OF SERVIUS TULLIUS. Italy adopts equipment from the Levant, better adapted to a crowded, hot country. The disadvantages of the older equipment may be deduced from the rear figure, with the inferior old Italic armament—globular helmet, pectoral and large oval shield (*scutum*).

The Hoplite in the foreground wears a Boeotian helmet and a two-piece breastplate, fixed by a belt (*cingulum*). Helmet, breastplate, shield and greaves all of bronze.

28

A Hoplite in the army of Servius Tullius

The sword is still awkwardly suspended,
and the shield, although an improvement,
can be bettered. The cuirasse is of metal
scales sewn on to leather, with shaped metal
shoulder-pieces.

THE BASIS REMAINS A FIGHT AT CLOSE QUARTERS

A SCENE AT AN ETRUSCAN FEAST. Here a
dancing woman intervenes at a feast to pre-
vent a conflict between an Etruscan spear-
man and an archer. Armour is still adapted
for spear-fighting, with the sword as a later
resource. Bowmen are rare, since really
strong bows are hard to make.

A SCENE AT AN ETRUSCAN FEAST

The richer citizen (*eques*) can afford a horse, but it is ineffective in Italian marsh or mountain, in contrast with the great plains. The round shield is the special *palma equestris*.

SO THE WEALTHY ROMANS IMPROVE BODY-ARMOUR

RORARIUS AND TRIARIUS OF CAMILLUS. By the time of Camillus (circa 396 B.C.) a great improvement has taken place in arms and tactics. The sword is better suspended; an oblong or oval shield gives better cover; a javelin increases the range of action, and gives new importance to the sword. But the poor still rely on swiftness for success. In the foreground is a *triarius* or heavy-armed infantryman, richly equipped. His general appearance is Greek, except for Roman oval *scutum* and Iberic sword. Behind him, the *rorarius*, or light-armed skirmisher, is the poorest of soldiers, armed with an ancient javelin (*verutum*), or sling and stones.

RORARIUS AND TRIARIUS OF CAMILLUS

A Gaulish chief, his helmet crested with a pair of wings. The large and powerful Gauls present new problems, and rigid discipline is required to deal with their reckless, unbridled courage.

AND EVEN FROM THE ITALIAN ALLY

AN INFANTRYMAN AT AN INN. The Allies (confederate cities) now begin to form an important part of the Roman army, but their equipment is less standardised. Here is a rich infantryman of the first-class. He wears an elaborate bronze helmet, Iberic sword, Gaulish coat-of-mail, bronze greaves, oval shield, and heavy javelin (*pilum*).

An infantryman at an inn

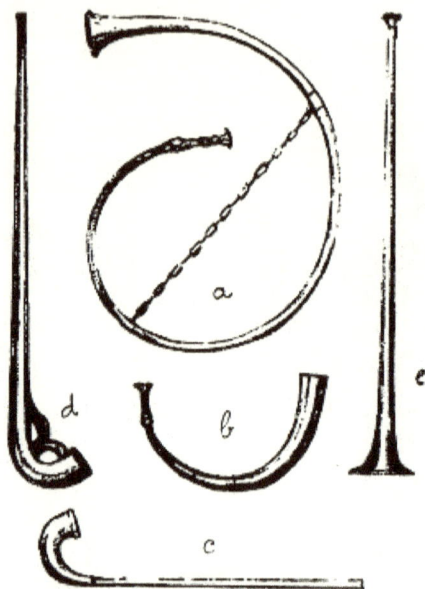

Military trumpets have various forms : (*a*) the *cornu*, (*b*) the *bucina*, (*c* and *d*) the *lituus*, peculiar to the cavalry, (*e*) the *tuba*.

PLAYED BY SPECIAL TRUMPETERS

THE *CORNICEN* OR TRUMPETER. A *cornicen* sounds the watches (*vigiliæ*) on the space behind the rampart of a frontier fort. In this illustration he is shown playing upon the *cornu*. The *cornu* and *tuba* were sounded together as the signal to attack.

The *Cornicen* or Trumpeter

AND INTRODUCE ORGANISED DISCIPLINE

To increase efficiency in drill and discipline,
the drill-master (*lanista*) is introduced from
the gladiators' schools. He teaches drill
and obedience to signals from the trumpet.
Here he marks the sand of the arena in
preparation for a combat, while one of the
gladiators announces the coming event by a
blast on the horn.

ADD TO THIS TRAINING IN SWORDMANSHIP

GLADIATORS. THE END OF THE COMBAT.
Gladiators reared in special schools were
rigidly drilled. Drill was first introduced
into the army by Rutilius in Gaul (117 B.C.)
to deal with northerners, and under the
Empire it became a regular feature. In
this picture the victor is a Samnite who has
overcome a Thracian; each is armed after
the manner of his people, and both—be it
noted—carry the rectangular shield adopted
later in the Roman army.

GLADIATORS. THE END OF THE COMBAT

Artillery, invented by fourth-century Greece, was adopted by the Romans on a large scale in the second century. This drawing was made from a catapult (*ballista*) reconstructed for Napoleon III by Verchère de Reffye. With a similar reconstruction by Major E. Schramm of Dresden it was possible to shoot some three hundred yards.

AND THE ROUTE MARCH

THE *IMPEDITUS*, OR FULLY-EQUIPPED FOOT SOLDIER. With drill came the route-march. Marius much improved the soldier's task by arranging the pack so that it could be carried on a pole, though hardly for long. Besides his own baggage, each soldier carried tools for pitching camp and raising earth-works. The infantryman was called *impeditus*, and in derision *mulus marianus*—the mule of Marius. Note the change in dress: there are no greaves; the tunic reaches to the knee; a thick cloak, dyed reddish-brown, and a woollen neck-cloth (*focale*) are worn, with hobnail sandals. The arms are a rectangular shield, an Iberic sword on the right thigh, a dagger (*pugio*) on left side, a cuirasse of scales or mail; a steel helmet, and two javelins.

THE *IMPEDITUS* OR FULLY-EQUIPPED FOOT SOLDIER

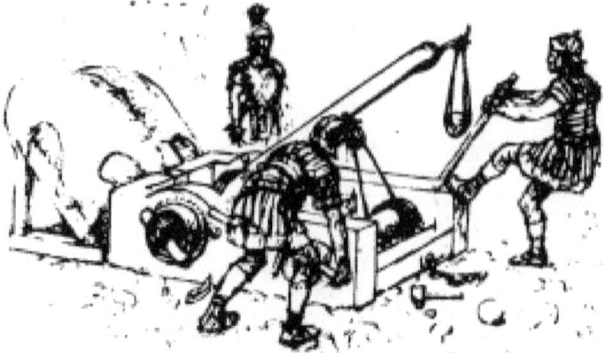

Here is the *onager*, the " wild ass," which
had a great " kick," or recoil. It was
worked by twisted rope, hair or sinew, but
had one arm only, unlike the *ballista*, which
had two. It was more dangerous to use,
being liable to burst, with disastrous consequences. With the reconstruction by
Verchère de Reffye stone balls were thrown
up to 120 yards.

UNITS RECEIVE REGULAR STANDARDS OR ENSIGNS

A STANDARD-BEARER IN THE FIELD. Until
the time of Marius, units had no regular
standard to which they might rally in battle.
When these were introduced they were
carried by a special standard-bearer (*signifer*), chosen for strength and valour, who
preceded the column on the march and took
his station in the hindmost rank of the
maniple during the fight. Over the helmet
and shoulders the skin of a wild beast was
worn to inspire terror. The arms included
an Iberic sword, a *lorica* of scales, and a
small oval shield. A strap of leather was
probably used to help in holding up the
standard.

A Standard-Bearer in the field

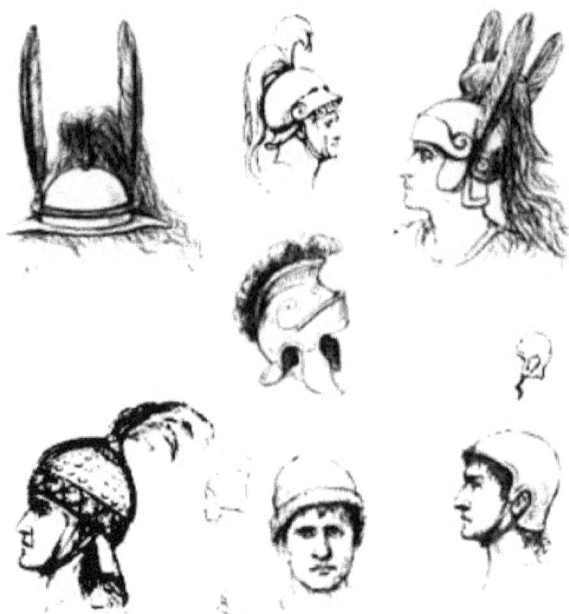

Older fashions still continue and there is much variation in ornamentation, from elaborate plumed helmets to leather and felt caps. Poverty or inexperience still fulfils its needs in the old way. The sailor, who is seen above in a woollen cap, never adopts armour at all.

WITH THE BEST TYPE OF EQUIPMENT

A LEGIONARY GUARDING CAPTIVES IN THE FIELD. He wears a distinctive Roman helmet with wide horizontal back peak, fine scale armour, a cuirasse over leather jacket; and leather breeches, adopted for colder climes. His shield is rectangular, and the Iberic sword is suspended from the military belt (*cingulum militare*), distinguished by the three overhanging leather ends; a dagger hangs from a separate belt on the left thigh.

A Legionary guarding captives in the field

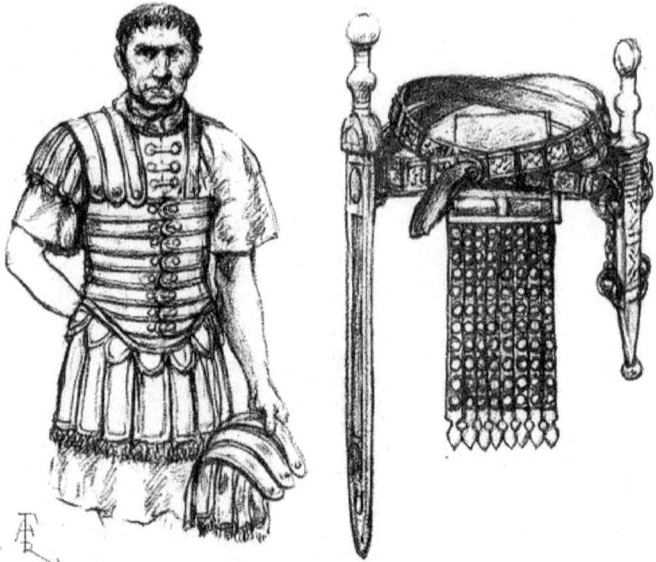

Another type of cuirasse is shown here, the *lorica segmentata* or articulated breast-plate, not quite so efficient as chain mail, but more easily made. On the right is the *cingulum militare*. The sword, shield and dagger became standardised by the 1st century A.D.

100 B.C.-1 B.C.

THERE STILL EXISTS OLDER TYPES

A HALT BY THE ROADSIDE. The two seated infantrymen making a meal by the wayside have the older type of shield and helmet, the cheek pieces of the latter lifted up for greater comfort. The standing figure wears a Romano-Corinthian helmet with a plume of horsehair, and a protective plate over his scale armour.

A HALT BY THE ROADSIDE

This was the latest type of legionary helmet at the opening of the 1st century A.D. Note that the crest is removed in action and used on parade only.

AGAIN, THE USE OF NON-ROMAN CAVALRY

AUXILIARY CAVALRY ATTACKING GERMAN TRIBESMEN. Since the rich-citizen-cavalry had meanwhile proved ill-disciplined and useless, the Romans were compelled to raise *auxilia*, corps of auxiliary cavalry from barbaric tribes; Spaniards and Numidians were the first favourites (2nd and 1st Centuries, B.C.) : then came the turn of the Gauls and Germans. The auxiliary in the picture carries the lance (*hasta*) and a broad two-edged sword (*spatha*). His gleaming brass helmet has an iron visor. Hexagonal shield, red leather tunic, and leather breeches complete his equipment. Legs and feet go bare.

AUXILIARY CAVALRY ATTACKING GERMAN TRIBESMEN

Light-infantrymen (*velites*) were also required to balance the legionary; they were
armed with a round shield and short light
javelins and wore a bear or wolf skin over
the helmet. Slingers (*funditores*) were
also much used; first Cretans and Balearic
Islanders, then northerners.

TENDS TO OBSCURE THE TRIUMPH OF STANDARDISATION

A LEGIONARY SENTRY. By the 1st Century
A.D., however, the armour of the legionary,
here seen on duty outside the guardroom,
has become completely standardised, the
only difference being in regimental crests
and *insignia*. This legionary is wearing a
true Roman helmet, the classic *cassis;* a
flexible breastplate, and a red cloak on his
back. The *gladius ibericus* hangs from his
left shoulder, and the military belt with its
apron of leather flaps over his tunic. In
his right hand is the *pilum*.

A LEGIONARY SENTRY

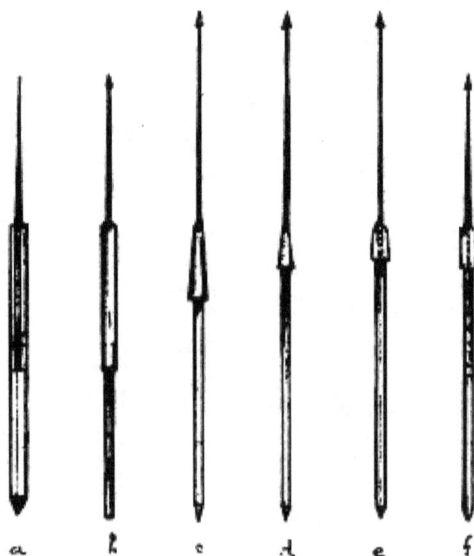

a   b   c   d   e   f

The *pilum* or javelin, thrown by the legionary before charging in battle, is most important. It has a soft nose which twists in the enemy's armour or shield and cannot be easily removed. The suggested reconstructions given above are by (*a*) Rustow; (*b*) Quicherat; (*c* and *d*) Lindenschmitt; (*e*) Schulten; (*f*) Couissin. There is no doubt about the general form.

THE DIFFERENCE NOW CONSISTS IN INSIGNIA

A CENTURION ON THE MARCH. The centurion was the lowest of the higher officials of the legion, but perhaps the best-known of legionary officers. He was chosen on his personal merits, physical and moral, and passed by regular promotion from cohort to cohort. He wears silvered armour, and a helmet bearing the transverse crest distinctive of his office; greaves decorate his legs. In his right hand he carries his official staff, the *vitis*, a vine staff, with which to flog recalcitrant soldiers.

A Centurion on the march

Each legion had its own armourers for standard repairs, but armour was issued from special factories in different parts of the Roman world, and each factory would produce its own type. This is an Attic helmet with a movable crest or plume of red and black feathers in two rows. The wearer has about his neck the *focale* or woollen muffler.

AS THE AUXILIARY CAVALRY ALSO

AT A POST-HOUSE. With the acquisition of northern provinces and the necessity for a standing garrison, the auxiliary cavalry came to be used largely for patrolling the great roads. Such a road, provided with a convenient posting station, for official use only, is shown here, with its varied scenes. The posting service was organised by Augustus for officials only, although permission to use it was sometimes given, as a rare privilege, to private travellers. Hostelries (*mansiones*) were provided on first-class roads. They were distant from each other a day's journey, and the interval was divided by smaller houses, *mutationes*, for change of horses. The post-house was invaluable for cavalry, and here a cavalry soldier is seen leading his lame horse to the *mansio*, where a veterinary surgeon may be found; stations so elaborately equipped were, of course, rare, and can have existed on few roads in Britain.

AT A POST-HOUSE

The cohorts or auxiliaries were stationed
in small forts. Above is a reconstruction
of the Saalburg fort, on the German
frontier near Homburg. Built under
Hadrian, it was partly restored by Kaiser
Wilhelm II. The large central building
is the headquarters (*praetorium*). Near the
gate, in front of it, is a pair of granaries
(*horrea*). All the tents and many large
camp buildings do not figure in this plan,
which indicates the shape and extent of the
enclosure.

AND IS STATIONED IN FORTS

A FORT IN CUMBERLAND. A view of Hard-
knott Fort, between Ambleside and Raven-
glass, a small post between two large forts,
which belongs to the age of Trajan, A.D.
98—117. Such forts as these replace in
Britain the earthworks of Agricola's time.
Their stone-built wall forms a rectangular
enclosure with rounded angles and four
gates. The fort has a regular street-plan.
Most of the space is taken by long parallel
barracks in rows, each for a *centuria* of
eighty men. The garrison is five-hundred
strong. A village has grown up beside the
fort, and in it the soldiers' families and
trades-folk live in half-timbered cottages,
often protected by an earthwork.

A FORT IN CUMBERLAND

This is a sailor at *Pons Aelius*, the Tyne
Bridge on Hadrian's Wall at Newcastle.
All important river-crossings of this sort
would be guarded by an auxiliary fort.

OUTSIDE A PERMANENT CAMP IN GERMANY. Auxiliary soldiers, on retiring from the service, often settle down with their families in the bazaar or village settlement outside the permanent camp, which they are forbidden to enter. Often these bazaars grow into large villages or even towns. At the end of the road, shown here beyond the bridge over the double fosse, stands the *porta decumana* with its two arches. The soldier in the foreground dictates a letter to a public letter-writer, in this case a Greek.

OUTSIDE A PERMANENT CAMP IN GERMANY

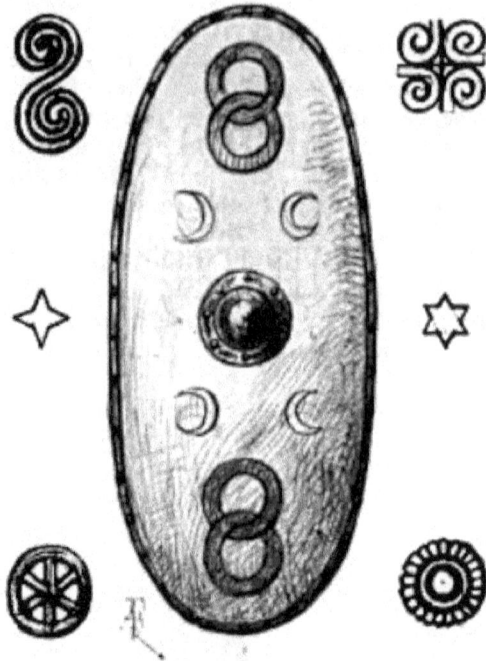

The oval shields of the auxiliary cavalry
bear emblems and symbols, sometimes of
magical origin, which differ remarkably
according to the unit. Illustrations of many
of these are preserved to us in the *Notitia
Dignitatum*, a fifth-century list of Imperial
Officials and their insignia.

AND OFTEN APPROACHED THAT OF THE LEGIONARY

AN AUXILIARY AT A FERRY ON THE TYNE.
An abundance of leather distinguishes the
equipment of this auxiliary, waiting for the
ferry, from that of the legionary, but the
pilum with which he is armed is essentially
the legionary's weapon. His pectoral is of
leather, an Iberic sword hangs from his left
shoulder, an apron belt is worn over short
leather breeches, and the rectangular *scutum*
has re-appeared.

AN AUXILIARY AT A FERRY ON THE TYNE

Roman policy encourages the auxiliary troops to employ the weapon (for example, this mace) which they were wont to use in their native land.

NOTABLY THE ARCHERS FROM THE EAST

ASIATIC ARCHERS AND SLINGERS. The Syrians and Palmyrenes, by age-old tradition, are skilled in using the bow, and provide a valuable series of auxiliary corps to the Roman army. The figure in the foreground here is based on a scene from the Dacian Wars (102-106 A.D.), as shown on Trajan's Column. In the background are the slingers, most of whom came from the Balearic Islands. Both bowmen and slingers are partly equipped in Roman fashion while retaining their native weapons.

ASIATIC ARCHERS AND SLINGERS

In the upper picture are *dorsarii*, or beasts of burden, of the time of Theodosius, with their conductors. Below, two soldiers of Tiberius rest beside a milestone on the Roman way.

ARTERIAL VEINS OF THE EMPIRE

A MESSAGE FOR THE COMMANDANT. A messenger has just reached the Commandant's house in an outlying fort. He is heavily cloaked, against bad weather, but delivers his message in an atmosphere of comfort which is by no means exceptional. His long, heavy, hooded cloak (*pœnula*), is closed across the chest, like the North African "burnous." The Commandant wears a light hooded cloak (*lacerna*), shorter than the *pœnula*, over a tunic adorned with two narrow purple bands as a mark of distinction. The *lacerna* is worn in the house instead of the cumbersome *toga*, reserved for out-of-doors.

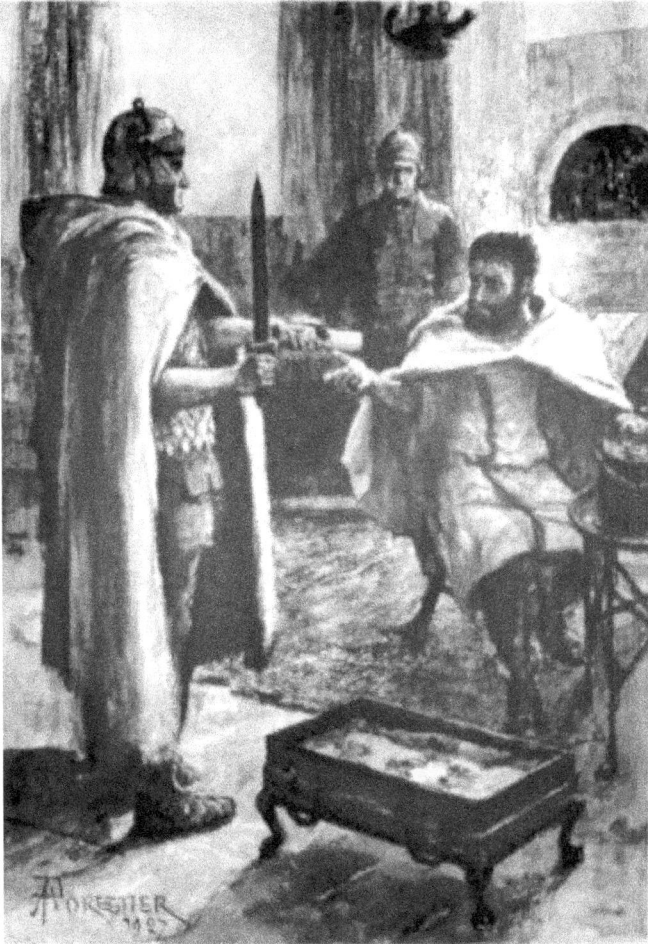

A MESSAGE FOR THE COMMANDANT

Another useful field-machine, the "tortoise,"
of Greek origin, used for providing cover
while filling up ditches or digging mines.
A similar machine was in use throughout
the Middle Ages.

IF SOMETIMES PROSAIC ENOUGH IN DETAIL

AN EMPEROR RECEIVES THE SUBMISSION
OF BARBARIAN CHIEFS. The chiefs are
doing obeisance in the field to the eagle,
the legionary standard. The Emperor sits
on a raised platform (*tribunal*) built of turf,
and is surrounded by his standards, officers
and trumpeters. *Lictors* stand on either
side, their *fasces* wreathed with laurels.

An Emperor receives the submission of Barbarian chiefs

Fleet-patrol is an important branch of Roman frontier activity; early instances of naval forces are the Nile and Danube flotillas; later the Channel fleets of Britain and Gaul. This is a sea-going bireme leaving Dover; she carries an emperor across the straits to Gessoriacum (Boulogne). River-boats were smaller.

OR BY LAND SHOULD BECOME

PATROLLING A NORTH-BRITISH FORT IN WINTER. A winter scene from Hadrian's wall. A member of the corps of Hamian Archers, stationed at Carvoran (Magnae), has turned out for action. Perhaps a hare in the snow is providing a tempting target and the possibility of some warm soup. The soldier wears a thick hooded cloak (*cucullus*) and, over his sandals, rough boots (*perones*) of untanned leather.

PATROLLING A NORTH-BRITISH FORT IN WINTER

The modelled cuirasse with its special sword-belt is the peculiar privilege of high commanders and Emperors. The greatest care is expended upon its production, and it ranks high as an artistic achievement.

DEFINITELY ORGANISED AS IN BRITAIN

A GENERAL LOOKS OUT FROM HADRIAN'S WALL. A frontier general, perhaps Platorius Nepos (the builder of the Wall itself) is looking out beyond Hadrian's Wall near Cawfields. In the background is a milecastle, one of the patrol-stations, which guarded sally-ports through the Wall. These stations enclose two barracks, capable of housing some eighty men.

70

A GENERAL LOOKS OUT FROM HADRIAN'S WALL

But frontier-walls, intended to keep out mass-troopers, fail to keep out massed invasions, and this is one of the causes of the disintegration of the Empire. Here such an invader, a German, is asking his way of a ploughman.

AND MILITARY COMMANDERS IN REVOLT

THE ENTRY OF CONSTANTINE INTO LONDON. No less dangerous is the tendency of provincial governors to declare themselves Emperors at the head of their armies. One of the most successful revolts is that of Carausius, an admiral of the Channel fleet in Britain. He becomes emperor of Britain for twelve years, and is succeeded by Allectus, but then the central government under Constantius Cæsar recovers the island. The illustration shows the entry of Constantine, son of Constantius, into London (*Londinium*), the biggest town in the Province. Guided by two pages, and followed by his staff, he rides between his life-guards (*Prætoriani*), who are armed only with large round shields and spears. Cavalry line the road; magistrates have come to the gate to receive the Emperor and precede him to the *Forum*. In the background is the northern or Bishop's gate, adorned with garlands.

THE ENTRY OF CONSTANTINE INTO LONDON

The *pilum* (*d*) gives way before the weapons of the auxiliary army. The *gaesum* (*a*) of Rhaetia, the javelins (*b*) and spears (*c*) of Spain, and the lance (*solliferrum*) (*e*) of Southern Gaul, come into their own.

IN FAVOUR OF AUXILIARIES AND NEW INVENTIONS

THE *CATAPHRACTUS* OR ARMOURED CAVALRY-MAN. Iron-mailed cavalry, though appearing occasionally in the early Empire, are not tested until the fourth century, when they are used by Maxentius against Constantine. The obvious defects of these "knights" are their weight and lack of mobility when unhorsed; the rider when armed has to be lifted on to his mount. The invention was quite unsuccessful. The armour is of square pieces of iron or brass, overlapping like scales. The whole body of the soldier is covered save that part of the thigh which grips the horse at a spot where there is a break in the animal's armour. The helmet fits closely round the neck, and the face is protected by a visor pierced with many holes.

THE CATAPHRACTUS OR ARMOURED CAVALRYMAN

The classic sense of fitness in ornamentation is amply typified by this simple cavalry standard (*vexillum*) of the Trajanic Age (A.D. 98-117), with its purple banner and gold fringe and gilded statue of victory.

To that of early Mediaevalism

THE EMPEROR STARTS THE GAMES. Nothing could be a greater contrast than this Constantian Emperor clad in full insignia, and giving the signal, a dropped kerchief (*mappa*), to start the games. A semi-oriental and barbaric conception of the Emperor has taken the place of the Labouring Hero inspired by duty, conceived by Marcus Aurelius. The consular dress of the Emperor consists of a modification of the *toga* worn with a long tunic, called *tunica palmata*. It is put on like a shawl, both ends crossing over the left shoulder, the longer being brought round from behind and thrown over the left arm. Part of the Imperial Court dress in Byzantium, it became the *pallium* of Christian bishops.

THE EMPEROR STARTS THE GAMES

On the other hand, the truly classic sense of dignity and beauty is well shown by these two helmets from Newstead near Melrose, and Ribchester near Preston, now in Edinburgh and London respectively. Both belong to the end of the first century, when old artistic ideals still possessed much influence.

To Barbaric Wilderness

SPANISH AND FRANK AUXILIARIES. A Spanish cavalryman, a ghost of a former age, is confronted by a fourth century Frankish soldier. The inability of the barbaric army to assimilate classical ideals was to prove one of the potent causes of the ruin of the Ancient World. The Spaniard is drawn from a grave-stone found in Burgundy, now in the Museum at Châlons-sur-Saône. The arms and equipment are similar to those of the horseman described on page 78. The Frankish soldier carries his native weapons—the axe (*francisca*) of peculiar shape worn in the belt is thrown with considerable effect,—a leather helmet reinforced with iron bands, and a cuirasse and thorax, both of skins dressed with the hair outside.

Spanish and Frank Auxiliaries

STILICHO, A VANDAL, THE ROMAN *MAGISTER UTRIUSQUE MILITIÆ.* Eventually the barbaric army, by which the Empire is defended, is itself unable to stave off its wilder cousins, but there are some valiant efforts. Stilicho, one of the most notable generals of the late Empire, supreme commander of both infantry and cavalry, is a Vandal. In the background of the picture are Hun auxiliaries, clothed in hauberks of mail. In the foreground stand a bodyguard, and a page holding the general's helmet. Stilicho's shield is splendidly decorated, and his helmet bears a crest of red feathers; his tunic and cloak (*paludamentum*) are of gold-embroidered cloth.

STILICHO, A VANDAL, THE ROMAN MAGISTER UTRIUSQUE MILITIAE

The Roman Soldier at War

Contents

The Roman Soldier at War

§ 1. EQUIPMENT AND TACTICS.

The early history of the Roman Army can only be traced by combining various forms of evidence. Tradition is of comparatively little value, since the authentic records of early Rome had perished before the annalists upon whose works we ultimately depend began to write; thus, for example, the battle-pieces inserted in Livy's history cannot be used as evidence and are not even consistent with his narrative. From archaeology and survivals we can infer that in the earliest period king and nobles rode to battle in chariots, and, as in Homeric warfare, met their enemies in single combat, while the common host were of small account. The *currus* in which the Roman *triumphator* rode in procession was the direct descendant of that in which the early kings had gone forth to war, just as his dress was copied from that of the monarch.

We shall see that the *Salii*, or 'dancing priests' of Mars, were charged with the care of the *ancilia*, or shields believed to have fallen from heaven, and that these were of the peculiar Mycenaean form with sides drawn in in the shape of a figure of eight; the 'spears of Mars' too, which were kept in his shrine, belonged to the equipment of the earliest of Rome's warriors. It is probable that this mode of fighting was learnt by the Romans from the Etruscans; bronze chariots have been found at several sites in Etruria, and early *terra-cotta* plaques are preserved which show the chieftain mounting his car. The *tensa* (Pl. XLIX) used in religious processions may give us some idea of its form.

According to Roman tradition, the army as organised by Romulus consisted of 3,000 footmen, 1,000 from each of the three tribes, commanded by three *tribuni militum*, and 300 horsemen (*celeres*) under three *tribuni celerum*. The numbers of the infantry have no claim upon our credence; but those of the cavalry must be examined more closely. In historical times the Roman *equites* (who eventually became a political rather than a military class) were organised in eighteen centuries; and six of these—called the *sex suffragia* or 'six voting-units'—enjoyed precedence over the rest. Tradition is confused as to the gradual increase in the number of *equites*, but it seems clear that the three centuries of Romulus were doubled, and that twelve were added when the reform ascribed to Servius Tullius took place. Now there is good evidence for the view that the *equites* of early Rome, were a force, not of cavalry, but of mounted infantry. Even in Livy's narrative this is implied.

More than once, in describing the wars of the fifth century B.C., he tells us that the *equites* 'dismounted' and attacked the enemy on foot; and where he speaks of the cavalry as throwing a hostile *phalanx* into confusion, he is no doubt following traditions which he did not fully understand. *Terra-cotta* plaques have been found in Rome which show horsemen with two chargers apiece; and these throw light on the statement of Roman antiquarians that in early times the *equites* went into battle 'with pairs of horses'. Not all of them, however; for one historian tells us that when 'Tarquinius' doubled the numbers of the cavalry, he gave to the *equites priores* two horses apiece: this implies that the *equites posteriores* had only one horse—a distinction which, as archaeological evidence shows, existed in Greece. Thus the 'six centuries' of early Rome contained both classes of horsemen.

We now come to the reform ascribed by Roman tradition to Servius Tullius, which was at once political and military. The accounts which we possess of this reform differ in detail, but agree touching the main feature of the new model—a *phalanx* of spearmen whose equipment was graduated according to their property. There were five classes, each of which was divided into a number of *centuriae* which, when the people met in assembly, served as voting-divisions. The equipment of the various classes was as follows. The first had full hoplite armour after the Greek model, spear and sword, helmet (*galea*), cuirass (*lorica*), greaves (*ocrae*), and round buckler (*clipeus*). The second class wore no cuirass, and used the semi-cylindrical shield (*scutum*) in place of the buckler. The third were without greaves. In Livy's account the fourth and fifth classes are light troops, the former being armed only with spear and dart, the latter with sling and stones; but Dionysius of Halicarnassus gives spear, sword, and shield to the fourth, dart and sling to the fifth. (The troops of the fourth and fifth classes were called *rorarii*.) There were other voting-divisions beside those of the army, also called *centuriae*—two of artificers (*fabri*), and one each of horn-blowers, trumpeters, and *accensi*, whose function is uncertain; and the *capite censi*, who comprised the *proletariate*, formed a century apart. The cavalry, as already explained, were organised in eighteen *centuriae*, which in voting took precedence of the rest. We can place no faith in the details of this reform. Many critics hold that the 'centuries' were from the first voting-divisions, not tactical units, and that the timocratic organisation of the assembly dates from the Republican epoch. However this may be, the fact is clear that at some period in their early history the Romans adopted the principle of the Greek hoplite *phalanx* of pikemen. The graduation of equipment in its various ranks according to census ratings is much more doubtful. The word *classis*, which in later times was applied to each of the five 'classes', originally denoted the *phalanx* as a whole; those who fought in it were called *classici*, the rest of the citizen body, who served as light troops, were *infra classem*.

The 'levy in arms' (*classis procineta*) was distinguished from the 'levy of sailors' (*classis navalis*) when Rome first formed a fleet; and later still the word classis was restricted to the sense of fleet when used without qualification. We cannot determine with certainty the date at which the Romans adopted the *phalanx*; there was a tradition that the '*phalanx* and shield of bronze' were used by the Etruscans and borrowed from them by the Romans in self-defence; and Servius Tullius, whether he was a historical character or not, represents a dynasty of Etruscan kings ruling in Rome. More than this we cannot say.

We can infer something about the early *phalanx* from the names which survived, though with altered meaning, in the later Roman army. In this the front ranks were called *hastati*, the next *principes*, and the reserve *triarii*. It is evident that the *principes* must originally have been the front rank; the view of Livy, who transfers to the fourth century B. C. the usage of a later time, is that the *hastati* were the younger men, who bore the brunt of the first onslaught, the *principes* those of maturer years; but this is clearly artificial. It is less easy to be certain why the *triarii* were called *pilani*, the *hastati* and *principes antepilani*.

It would be natural to assume that the *phalanx* was armed with the *hasta*, the reserve with the javelin or *pilum*, of which we shall presently speak; in that case the equipment of the several ranks must have been exactly reversed in the Middle Republic, for the *hastati* and *principes* were then armed with the *pilum*, the *triarii* with the *hasta*. But the word *pilanus* seems to be derived, not from *pilum*, but from *pilus*, for the chief centurion of the *triarii* was called the 'centurion of the *primus pilus*'; and *pilus* appears to signify a body of troops drawn up in close formation, as, no doubt, were the reserves of the Roman legion.

It was not, however, to the hoplite *phalanx* that Rome owed her triumphs. The army which conquered the world was armed, not with the spear, but with the javelin, and disposed not as a *phalanx* but in companies (*manipuli*) of two centuries each or 120 men. We have no conclusive evidence as to the date of these changes, but such indications as we possess point to the fourth century B. C. We are told by Plutarch that Camillus, the conqueror of Veii, brought about the payment of the citizen-troops, who had hitherto served during the campaigning months at their own expense, but were compelled by the siege of Veii to take part in winter operations; and that he also introduced the *scutum*, or semi-cylindrical shield, in place of the *clipeus*, or round buckler, and the javelin, or *pilum*. Livy more cautiously states that the *scutum* was adopted 'after the Romans had begun to receive pay', and that at the same time the close order of the *phalanx* was replaced by the more open *manipular* formation.

There was, however, a different tradition, preserved to us in an anonymous Greek fragment possibly based on the history of Fabius Pictor, who was a contemporary of Hannibal. According to this writer the *scutum* and *pilum* replaced the *clipeus* and *hasta* during the Samnite Wars; and it was then, too, that Rome first formed an efficient cavalry force, having hitherto depended mainly on infantry. The passage has been quoted in support of the view mentioned above, that the *equites* of early Rome were mounted footmen rather than true cavalry; but it is quite as important for the history of the equipment of the Roman foot-soldier. The tradition which it enshrines gains weight from the phrase which Sallust puts into the mouth of Julius Caesar, 'we borrowed the armour and weapons of our soldiers from the Samnites'; and the *scutum* was part of the equipment of the gladiator called a 'Samnite'.

As for the *pilum*, it is by various writers assigned to Etruscans, Iberians, Sabines, and Samnites as a national weapon; and the last-named people have the best claim if, as seems likely, it was supported by Varro. The form of the *pilum* is well known to us, both from the description of Polybius and from extant examples. The weapon described by Polybius had two parts, the wooden shaft three cubits (4½ feet) long, and the barbed iron point, which was of the same length but extended half-way down the shaft, so that the whole length of the *pilum* was about 6¾ feet. Among the *pila* discovered in modern excavations those found at Numantia, dating from the famous siege which ended in 138 B. C., naturally correspond most closely with Polybius's description. Marius, who armed the *triarii* with the *pilum* instead of the *hasta*, and thus gave to the whole legion a uniform equipment, ordered one of the two rivets by which the point was fixed to the shaft to be made of wood. This broke when the *pilum* pierced an enemy's shield, and as the point became bent it was impossible for the enemy to make use of the weapon. For the *pilum* described by Polybius a lighter weapon was substituted in the course of the first century B. C., the various forms of which are illustrated by finds made in Caesar's lines of circumvallation at Alesia (Alise-Ste-Reine). The iron head was shortened to 3 feet and less, and was fixed in the shaft by means of a tang about 8 inches long; the base was reinforced and took the shape of a truncated pyramid, while the point was either conical, pyramidal, barbed, or heart-shaped (Fig. 35a). As used in Imperial times the *pilum* was even lighter, as we see from examples found in the camps on the Rhine.

Polybius mentions a 'heavy' *pilum* as well as the light one of which we have traced the development; and there are several references in ancient historians to the *pilum murale*, which was chiefly used in siege-warfare by the defenders of walled cities. What this was has been shown by recent discoveries at the camp of Haltern in Westphalia, which is of early Imperial date. Here were found a number of wooden weapons, with sharp points at either end and a thin section in the middle by which they could be grasped, as in Fig. 35. The shape is that of an ancient pestle, which was called *pilum* by the Romans and gave its name to this weapon (which we find described, though not named, by a Greek writer on siege-warfare). The length of the *pila muralia* found at Haltern averages about 5 feet 8 inches; the central part is about 7 inches long.

The introduction of the *pilum*, which was hurled by the legionaries before charging the enemy at the sword-point, determined the character of Roman tactics, and put an end to the *phalanx*, which finds no place in the description of the Roman military system by Polybius. The legion in his time consisted of the heavy-armed troops, *hastati* (1,200), *principes* (1,200), and *triarii* (600), who were all equipped alike, except that the *triarii* still carried the *hasta*, and the light troops or *velites* (1,200). The defensive armour of the heavy troops consisted in the helmet with tall crest, the *lorica* or leathern jerkin, over which the common soldier wore a metal 'heart-protector' and the rich a cuirass of chain-mail, and the *scutum*, or oblong shield, about 4 feet long by

2½ feet broad, which was built upon a wooden framework with cloth and calf-skin and bent into a semi-cylindrical shape. For offence the legionary was armed with the *pilum* and Spanish sword, worn at the right side. This had replaced the Gallic sword, which the Romans had adopted in their wars with the northern invaders.

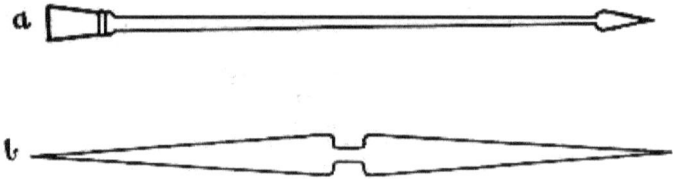

FIG. 35.   (*a*) **Iron point of** *pilum*.   (*b*) *Pilum murale*.

The Gallic sword had a long blade with a rounded point, used for cutting only; the Spanish *gladius* was a short, cut-and-thrust weapon, used in the hand-to-hand fight which followed the discharge of the *pilum*. The *velites*, according to Polybius, were armed with sword, darts (in Latin writers *veruta* or *gaesa*), and the light shield known as the *parma*. They are not, however, mentioned after the Jugurthine War, and the legion henceforth consisted solely of heavy infantry all armed alike; its full strength was raised by Marius to 6,000.

It is not until the closing years of the Republic that the monuments come to our aid in picturing the equipment of the Roman soldier; from thence onward we have, in historical reliefs and portraits on tombstones, abundant materials. The earliest monument of importance is a relief in the Louvre which shows a victorious general offering the *suovetaurilia* for the purification of his army. It is generally believed that he is Cn. Domitius Ahenobarbus, who built a temple to Neptune in the Campus Martius about 35-32 B.C. (The relief must in any case be assigned to this period, even if, as some hold, the subject is an earlier Domitius, who defeated the Allobroges in 121 B.C.)

The soldiers wear the high-crested helmet and coat of chain-mail described by Polybius, the short sword hangs at the right side, and the *scutum* is oval in shape with an iron band running down the centre. The commander wears a metal cuirass with lappets, such as those which we see in Imperial portraits: the finest extant example is that worn by Augustus in the statue of Prima Porta (Pl. LXIII).

The tactics of the Roman legion are not clearly explained by ancient writers. The open '*manipular*' formation which replaced the *pha-*

lanx is described by Livy (viii. 8) in a passage which, though obscurely expressed, appears to indicate that the thirty *maniples* of the legion were drawn up in three lines—*hastati, principes*, and *triarii*—in a chessboard pattern (*quincunx*), in order that those of the rear lines might be able to advance and fill the gaps made by the fight. It is very hard to see how this can have been put into practice, and it has been supposed that the *quincunx* belonged to the order of march (*agmen*), and not to the order of battle (*acies*).

From the time of Marius onwards the *cohort* of three *maniples* appears as the tactical unit in all descriptions of battles; and from the writings of Caesar and his officers it appears that the usual battle formation was the *triplex acies*, in which there were four *cohorts* in the first line and three in the second and third. The *simplex acies* was scarcely used except in defence of a fortified camp, and the *duplex* and *quadruplex* only when the nature of the ground required it. It has been contended that the formation of the *acies triplex* was open, so that the *cohorts* of the second line could fill the intervals between those of the first; but Caesar supplies no evidence of this, and the intervals were probably small.

The depth of the *cohort* was normally eight file; Pompey's *cohorts* at Pharsalus were drawn up ten deep, but this was unusual. We know little of the handling of large bodies of troops. The rule under the Republic was that the legions occupied the centre of the line, the 'auxiliaries' the 'wings'—hence they were called *ala sinistra* and *ala dextra sociorum*. On the extreme left was the cavalry of the allies, on the right the Roman *equites*, so long as they continued to exist. Cato in a tract, *de re militari*, copied by the later writer Vegetius, distinguished various battle formations—the unbroken front (*fronte longa*), the *acies obliqua* in which one of the wings led the advance, and the *acies sinuata* in which the centre was held back while both wings advanced. Again, the centre might be pushed forward in a crescent formation (as was done by Hannibal at Cannae) or in the wedge-like *cuneus*. If the enemy adopted these tactics, they were met by the V-shaped *forfex*. Caesar uses *orbis* of the formation adopted when a force was attacked on all sides, where in modern times a square is formed.

We have much fuller information about the organisation of the standing army of the Empire. The legions were no longer raised afresh for each campaign, as they had been in the days of the citizen levy, when two consular armies, each of two legions, had once formed the normal field force, (this number was of course largely exceeded in the great wars, in the second Punic War, for example, as many as twenty-seven were in the field at once); nor were they enlisted in the service of the individual commander and bound to him by the military oath (*sacramentum*) as long as his command lasted and no longer (as in the period of the Civil Wars, which were practically fought by mercenary bands), but were permanent corps retaining their numbering and titles under successive emperors, and often remaining in the same frontier camps for a considerable number of years.

Each legion still had ten *cohorts* and sixty centuries, but the first *cohort* contained 1,000 men and the others probably 500 each; the maniple continued to exist, as we shall find in considering the ensigns and encampments, and the old terms *hastati, principes*, and *triarii* (or rather *pili*) were retained in order to express the order of seniority of the centurions, who rose gradually from the command of the junior (*posterior*) century of *hastati* of the tenth *cohort* to the position of *primus pilus*, *i.e.* the *pilus prior* of the first *cohort*. (The centurions of the first *cohort* were called *primi ordines*). A small force of 120 mounted men (*equites legionis*) was attached to each legion. The legion was under the command of a *legatus legionis*, to be distinguished from the *legatus Augusti pro praetore*, who had the control of the whole military force stationed in a province, and corresponds with the modern army-corps commander, while the *legatus legionis* is to be compared with a general of division. The staff of the *legatus legionis* consisted of the six *tribuni militum* and the *praefectus castrorum* or 'quartermaster', whose importance grew steadily until in the third century he supplanted the *legatus*.

At the close of the Civil Wars the legions under arms numbered about fifty: Augustus retained eighteen, and the number was increased to twenty-five at the close of his reign. The addition of two legions by Claudius, one by Nero, and two by Galba, made the total thirty, which remained unaltered until the time of Septimius Severus, who enrolled the three 'Parthian' legions. The legions were distinguished by numbers—several of which were duplicated, since Augustus allowed those raised by his fellow *triumvirs* to retain the numeration belonging to them in the armies to which they had belonged—and by titles severally derived from their place of origin or service or from the name of an emperor or commander associated with their history; thus the *Legio XXII Deiotariana*, which served in Egypt, was formed of the Galatian levies of King Deiotarus.

The equipment of the Imperial Army is best illustrated by the monuments of the second century, and above all the reliefs of Trajan's

Column (cf. Plate XIII), which present a picture confirmed in every detail by finds such as those made in the camp of Carnuntum on the Danube, or in the frontier forts of Northern Britain and the Rhine. The cuirass worn by the legionary soldier appears in three forms, all of which are seen on one of the relief-panels from a monument of Marcus Aurelius used in the decoration of the Arch of Constantine (Pl. XXXVI).

The most usual is that which has been called *lorica segmentata*, although the name has no ancient authority. It was composed of a breastplate and backplate of iron, below which were worn iron hoops encircling the body and fastened with hinges at the back, while the shoulders were protected by similar strips. The strips found at Carnuntum vary in width from 2 to 3 inches. Portions of an iron cuirass of this kind with brass mountings were found at Newstead. We first see this cuirass—which is not mentioned in literary sources—on the Column of Trajan, and it is very common on second-century monuments; *e.g.* it is worn by the guardsmen who take part in the *decursio* represented on the base of the Column of Antoninus Pius (Pl. XLVI-II). A leathern jerkin was worn beneath it.

The coat of chain-mail (*lorica hamis conserta, ex anulis ferrea tunica*) is often represented on the monuments, and fragments of such have been found. There is also a third type, formed of metal scales (*squamae*) strung together in rows, which is usually shown as worn by officers: we are told by Cassius Dio that it was used by the praetorians in his time, until Macrinus lightened their equipment. Over the cuirass was worn the *balteus* or baldric, by which the sword was hung, and the waist was girt with the *cingulum militiae*, a leathern girdle studded with metal plates, from which hung a kind of apron formed by strips of leather as a protection for the abdomen. The helmet had various forms, and was made of iron, bronze, or brass, with padding. The simplest was a plain hemispherical cap of metal, prolonged at the back for the protection of the neck, with hinged cheek-pieces. More elaborate examples have raised mountings, notably a band of metal round the front which forms a peak, and many are decorated with reliefs.

★★★★★★

Beside the armour used in actual warfare, the Roman cavalry wore light tournament armour for the purpose of certain evolutions and exercises. To this belonged the vizor helmets with padded masks—some of them fine works of art—of which a number have been found, as for example at Newstead. Arrian describes these exercises, which were of Celtic origin.

★★★★★★

On the Column of Trajan, the helmets of the legionaries are surmounted by a crest or metal ring. The shield was either semi-cylindrical—the *scutum* proper, though smaller than that used in Republican times—hexagonal, or oval, this last being generally used by 'auxiliaries' In the centre was a raised boss or *umbo* bearing various ornamental devices, of which the thunderbolt is the commonest. It was made of wood covered with leather, and bound together with a metal framework and mountings, often in the shape of ribs attached to the *umbo*.

As a mark of distinction, certain ornaments were conferred on Roman soldiers which were called the *dona militaria*. These decorations are mentioned by Polybius, who tells us that they were bestowed by the commander in an assembly of the army, and that the soldier who wounded an enemy received a lance—the *hasta pura* of later authorities, which was a shaft without a point; while he who killed one and brought back his spoils received a bowl (*patera*) if a foot-soldier and a bowl if a cavalry-man. In Livy's narrative other decorations are mentioned, such as the *armilla* or bracelet, the *torques* or twisted necklace, such as was worn by the Celtic peoples and doubtless found its way to Some from the spoils of defeated Gauls; and minor ornaments such as chains (*catellae*) and brooches (*fibulae*).

More important were the crowns (coronae) of various kinds, differing according to the exploits by which they were earned. Setting aside the *corona obsidionalis*, a wreath of grass bestowed upon the deliverer of a beleaguered army, of which a few instances are recorded in Republican history, and the *corona triumphalis*, or bay-wreath worn by the *triumphator*, the crowns regularly bestowed on Roman soldiers were:

(*a*) the *corona civica*, a wreath of oak-leaves worn by one who had saved the life of a comrade;

(*b*) the *corona navalis* (also *c. classica* or *rostrata*), adorned with representations of ship's prows, given to the man who first boarded an enemy's ship;

(*c*) the *corona muralis*, in the form of a city wall, for the leader of a storming-party;

(*d*) the *corona vallaris*, in the form of a rampart, earned by the soldier who first entered an enemy's camp;

(*e*) the *corona aurea*, a plain gold crown given for distinguished

M. Aurelius delivering an *allocutio*.   *Anderson.*

bravery in the field.

Lastly, the *vexillum* was a small flag with silver mountings.

In Republican times these decorations retained their original significance. Pliny tells us that L. Siccius Dentatus received 18 *hastae purae*, 25 *phalerae*, 83 *torques*, 160 *armillae*, and 26 *coronae* of various kinds; and though the tale is legendary, it illustrates the freedom with which such marks of distinction were conferred. Under the Empire these orders, as we may call them, were made subject to definite rules depending on the rank of the recipients; these we can to some extent infer from the numerous inscriptions in which they are mentioned. We observe a distinction between the minor decorations—*armillae, phalerae,* and *torques*—and those of greater value, *coronae, hastae purae,* and *vexilla.*

The minor decorations were never given to officers, the greater ones seldom (the *vexillum* never) to private soldiers. *Centurions* hold an intermediate position. They received both the minor decorations and *coronae*, but rarely the *hasta pura* and never the *vexillum*. Fig. 86 shows the tombstone of one M. Caelius, centurion of the eighteenth legion, who lost his life when that corps was cut to pieces in the defeat of Varus by the Germans (*A. D.* 9). He wears *armillae* on both arms, *phalerae* decorated with Gorgon's heads and fastened on a framework upon his breast, *torques* suspended on either shoulder, and the *corona civica*. (In his left hand he carries the *vitis* or 'vine-staff', the symbol of the centurion's authority). This is a typical case. *Praefecti* and *tribuni* usually received one of each of the higher decorations, but sometimes two. *Legati*, if of *quaestorian* rank, could earn three *coronae*, two *hastae* and two *vexilla*; if of *praetorian*, three of each kind; if of consular standing, four. It was apparently usual for the three minor and three higher decorations to be granted simultaneously, as their significance had become conventional.

Besides the citizen infantry of the legions, the Romans employed contingents drawn from their allies, under the name of *auxilia*. Up to the close of the Social War these were furnished mainly by the Italian communities, although, for example, corps of archers and slingers were raised further afield; but when Italy was enfranchised, her inhabitants became liable for service in the legions and the *auxilia* were formed only by foreign contingents. We know little as to their organisation in the time of Caesar and the Civil Wars; under the Empire they formed regiments (*cohortes*) generally bearing their national designation (*cohortes Gallorum, Hispanorum, &c.*) recruited and quartered in the

Fig. 36. Tombstone of M. Caelius, centurion of the eighteenth legion.

various subject territories. (A few such corps were raised by voluntary enlistment among the Roman citizens of Italy and the provinces, and were called *cohortes civium Romanorum voluntariorum*).

The nominal strength of these regiments was either 500 (*cohors quingenaria*) or 1,000 (*cohors miliaria*), and some were exclusively composed of infantry (*cohortes peditatae*), whilst others had mounted sections (*cohortes equitatae*). They were at first lightly armed after their national fashion; but in process of time they became assimilated—with some exceptions—to the citizen troops in equipment. The revolt of Civilis on the Rhine (*A.D.* 69-70) opened the eyes of the Romans as to the danger of entrusting native troops with the defence of their own abodes, and henceforward the *auxilia* were transplanted for service in distant parts of the Empire.

Thus, we find in the West corps of archers (*cohortes sagittariorum*) recruited in the East, chiefly in Syria and the neighbouring lands. Such archers are more than once represented on Trajan's Column, as in Fig. 37, where they wear a conical helmet with cheek- and neck-pieces, a long tunic reaching to the ankles, a leathern jerkin with serrated edge, and a wrist-guard on the left forearm, and are armed with a sword as well as the bow. Cichorius believes that the corps here represented was of Palmyrene origin; and we find a *numerus* (*v. infra*) of Palmyrenes garrisoned in Dacia. In another scene the archers wear the *lorica squamata*.

Generally speaking, the regular *cohortes auxiliariae* were equipped with a short tunic, over which was worn a jerkin like that of the archer in Fig. 37, breeches, a neck-cloth (*focale*), *caligae*, and a round helmet crowned by a ring, and armed with an oval shield (sometimes a *scutum*) and sword; in fact, the costume of the cavalry-man in Fig. 40 is practically identical with that of the auxiliary infantry. There were, however, also irregular corps, known as *numeri*, which preserved their national equipment. The clubman shown in Fig. 38 (from Trajan's Column) is naked to the waist and wears only a pair of breeches, the upper part of which is rolled and girt at the waist, and is armed with sword and shield as well as the club (which was studded with nails); he is thought to be of German stock. The slinger (*funditor*) and stone-thrower (*libritor*) are shown working in conjunction (Fig. 39), just as we find them in two passages of Tacitus where they are mentioned (*Ann.* ii. 20, xiii. 39).

We know little of the equipment of the Roman cavalry in early times. Polybius tells us that they were clothed only with a light tunic (which cannot mean a 'loin-cloth' but a garment girt at the waist), and

Fic. 37. Palmyrene archer (from Trajan's Column).

Fig.38. German clubman (from Trajan's Column).

Fig. 39. *Funditor* and *libritor* (from Trajan's Column).

armed with a light spear and shield 'in the shape of a sacrificial cake', but that in later times the Greek equipment was adopted, i.e. cuirass, lance with pointed ferule, and heavy shield.

From Livy we gather that they were also armed with the Spanish sword. The citizen cavalry consisted partly of the younger members of the eighteen *centuriae* already mentioned, who were furnished with horses at the public cost (*equites equo publico*), partly of volunteers who supplied their own horses (*equites equo private*). Three hundred of these were assigned to each legion and divided into ten squadrons (*turmae*) of thirty each. But in the course of the second Punic War the cavalry furnished by the Italian allies of Rome came to outnumber the citizen force, and this latter ceased to be of importance and in time disappeared; those qualified for service on horseback were employed only for staff duties.

More than this, the place of the citizen cavalry was taken not only, nor chiefly, by allied contingents from Italy, but by non-Italian corps, for the most part recruited in Spain and Africa. This practice dates from the second Punic War, and, as it seems, was first employed on a large scale by Scipio Africanus. These *auxilia* become increasingly important during the second century B. C, and after the Social War and the enfranchisement of Italy which followed it constitute the whole mounted force of Rome. From this force were drawn the 300 *equites* still assigned to each legion during the last century of the Republic; but the main body of allied horsemen was usually divided into two portions and placed on the wings (*alae*), and hence the cavalry regiments formed in Imperial times, which varied in strength from 500 (in practice 480) to 1,000 men, bore the name of *alae*. (The *cohortes equitatae* contained a mounted section of the same class as the alae; the *equites legionis*, now reduced to 120, were Roman citizens, not auxiliaries).

The equipment of these 'auxiliary' horsemen is illustrated by many scenes from Trajan's Column, from which Fig. 40 is taken. The *eques* wears a leathern jerkin (*lorica*) over a tunic and drawers, a round helmet with cheek-pieces, and a knotted kerchief round his neck; he is armed with an oval shield, a sword hangs at his right side, and though his lance is not rendered plastically it was doubtless, like so many details in these reliefs, shown in painting. (The sword carried by the auxiliaries, called the *spatha*, had a longer and narrower blade than the *gladius* of the legionary. It was probably a Celtic weapon). The fringed saddle-cloth is clearly seen. The irregular cavalry employed by

Fig. 40. Roman auxiliary cavalry-man (from Trajan's Column).

Fig. 41. Moorish irregular cavalry-man (from Trajan's Column).

the emperors are also portrayed on the column. Fig. 41 shows one of the Moorish horsemen who, as we know, did good service in the Dacian Wars under their *sheikh*, Lusius Quietus, afterwards disgraced by Hadrian. They are easily recognised by their elaborate ringlets of hair; they are clad only in the tunic, and ride bare-backed. Their oval shields are shown, but not their weapons of offence.

The *catafractarii*, or mailed horsemen, of whom we read in inscriptions, were borrowed from the East, where we find them in the service of the Parthians. In the third century *A.D.* the cavalry, which had hitherto been of secondary importance in the Imperial Army, was reorganised by Gallienus, and in some degree supplied the lack of a 'striking force'. More important reforms were, however, introduced by Diocletian, who separated from the garrison army of the frontiers (*limitanei, riparienses*) a permanent field-force, destined to accompany the emperor or one of his colleagues in offensive warfare, and hence called *palatini* or *comitatenses*.

In the *Notitia Dignitatum* we possess an army list of the close of the fourth century, from which the names and number of the various corps may be learnt; but the details of their organisation remain obscure in many points. It is certain, however, that the legions, which were largely increased in number (there were about 170 under the new system), were at the same time greatly reduced in strength, probably becoming battalions of 1,000 men instead of the brigades of the early Empire.

§ 2. ENSIGNS.

According to a tradition which may be as old as Varro, Romulus himself gave the Roman army its first ensigns in the form of bundles of hay (*manipuli*) fixed on poles, which served as rallying-points for the sections. It is evident that this is a fiction intended to explain the use of the word *manipulus* in the sense of a tactical unit; but it points to the fact that such an unit existed from early times and was provided with a standard or *signum* by which its evolutions were directed. Thus, in Livy the word *signum* is used almost as the equivalent of *manipulus*. The same connexion between *manipulus* and *signum* is constantly implied by Caesar and Tacitus, although in the inscriptions of the Empire the *cohort* and *century* only are mentioned.

We shall see, however, that in barracks each *maniple* of two *centuries* had its separate quarters, and Tacitus speaks of it frequently as a tactical formation. Furthermore, it is clear that only one kind of *signum* was used in the legions, and therefore that it belonged to the *maniple* alone and not to the *cohort* and *century*. The *praetorians*, like the legions, had their *manipuli* and *signa*; and the monuments—especially the Column of Trajan and the historical reliefs of the second century, (on Pl. XXXVII is reproduced a relief of M. Aurelius, used in the decoration of the attic of the Arch of Constantine, upon which both legionary and *praetorian signa*, as well as a *vexillum*, are shown)—enable us to distinguish clearly the ensigns both of the legions and of the guard. Both consist in a lance with a point below by which it could be fixed in the ground.

Close to the top of the shaft (which was plated with silver) was a cross-piece of wood, from the ends of which hung purple ribbons ending in silver ivy-leaves. The shaft was adorned with a number of decorations, by the nature of which the legionary *signa* are distinguished from those of the *praetorians*. At the top of the legionary standard we find sometimes a small flag or *vexillum* with an oval shield fastened thereon, sometimes an open hand (which has been explained as symbolical of fidelity and therefore appropriate to such legions as bore the title *pia fidelis*, but is perhaps merely a talisman to avert ill-fortune), sometimes an eagle enclosed within a wreath; but the main ornament consists in a series of saucer-shaped disks.

There can be no doubt that the decorations found on legionary ensigns are strictly analogous to the *dona militaria* bestowed on individuals; and it will be remembered that, according to Polybius, a *patera* was bestowed on the soldier who brought back an enemy's spoils. This term would precisely describe the decorations of the legionary *signa*. It appears from coin-types that the *signum* also bore a plate which indicated the unit to which it belonged; and both coins and an extant example show that the animal symbols proper to the legion were likewise attached to the *signum*. Below the decorations we find a half-moon, which like the hand was regarded as a charm against ill-luck, and ornaments in the form of tassels.

The *signa* of the *praetorian* guard are easily distinguished from those just described. The uppermost portion shows much the same variety as that of the legionary ensigns; but the decorations consist, not in *paterae*, but in *coronae* of various kinds alternating with medallion portraits which cannot be identified in the representations which we possess, but obviously represent the emperor and other members of the reigning house. The *coronae* are generally simple *coronae aureae*, but we also find the *corona muralis* and *corona vallaris*. These orders were reserved

Anderson.

M. Aurelius receiving the homage of barbarian captives.

for the *cohorts* of the guards, and thus a distinction was drawn precisely parallel to that which we found in the case of the *dona militaria* conferred on individual soldiers. The medallion portraits or imagines indicate the attachment of the guards to the person of the emperor. Occasionally we also find statuettes of divinities, such as Victory (on a relief of M. Aurelius) or Jupiter (on a fragment in the Lateran), adorning the *signa* of the guard. On the Arch of Septimius Severus are represented *signa* of exceptional form in that medallions and *paterae* are seen side by side. I conjecture that these belong to the *legiones Parthicae* raised by Severus, which stood in a specially close relation to the emperor (who had disbanded the existing *praetorian cohorts* on his entry into Rome), and may therefore have obtained the coveted privilege of adorning their ensigns with portraits of their rulers.

It was by means of the *manipular signa* which we have described that the tactical unity of the sections was maintained and their movements directed; hence the great variety of expressions, such as *signa ferre, referre, constituere, movere, tollere, ad laevain ferre, retro recipere* and the like. Unfortunately, we have no means of determining where the *signum* was carried. It is beyond doubt that in marching order the *signiferi* or standard-bearers preceded their *maniples*; but in actual combat their place seems to have been in the rear of the first line. Livy often uses the term *antesignani* to describe the *maniples* of the *hastati* (which he also calls *prima signa*). and this would seem to imply that the *signa* were in rear of them during an engagement; but it is just possible that *signa* of a different kind are meant. In Caesar the word *antesignani* bears a different meaning, and denotes a picked troop of light-armed legionaries who skirmished in front of the line of battle in co-operation with the cavalry. (An inscription found in the armoury of the camp at Lambaesis distinguishes *arma antesignana*, and *postsignana*).

The costume of the *signiferi* in the second century *A. D.* is well known to us from the monuments. They were clad in a tunic and leathern jerkin and were armed with the sword, but in place of a helmet they wore a head-dress made of a lion's skin, probably with a metal lining. The words of command were directed to them, being given by the general to the trumpeters (*tubicines*), from whom it was passed to the horn-blowers (*cornicines* and *bucinatores*). These are shown on the Column of Trajan with the same headdress as the *signiferi*.

Besides the *signa* which we have described, there were other ensigns, not used for tactical purposes, but corresponding rather to the colours of our modern regiments. Pliny tells us that in the early Republic each legion had five standards—the eagle, wolf, minotaur, horse, and bear, which it has been thought may have been the *signa* carried in rear of the *hastati*; but that shortly before the time of Marius the eagle only had come to be used in action, and that Marius abolished the rest. Whatever truth there may be in this statement, it is at least certain that from his time onwards the eagle (*aquila*) was the symbol of the legion, the loss of which was an indelible disgrace and entailed the disbandment of the corps. The eagle was, in Republican times, of silver; under the Empire, of gold; in its beak was a thunderbolt, and it is sometimes represented with the *corona*, as a decoration conferred on the legion, encircling its wings. It was carried on a pole ending in a kind of capital by the *aquilifer* (whose equipment was that of the legionary), but the *primipilus* was responsible for its safe keeping. Thus, while it was carried at the head of the legion on the march, its place was by the first *cohort* in battle.

Although the other animal figures named by Pliny fell into dis-use, the legions of the Empire were each provided with a symbolical ensign of this kind. It has already been mentioned that these symbols adorned the *manipular signa*; thus the head of a wild goat (*capricornus*) is shown on a grave-relief discovered at Mainz, and similar figures are common on the coins (*e.g.* those of the Severi and Gallienus). The simplest explanation of these appears to be that they are astrological. Thus, the legions in the army of Augustus which owed their creation to Julius Caesar, bear the token of the Bull, and Taurus is the sign of the month sacred to Venus, the ancestress of the Julian house.

Those raised by Augustus himself carry the Capricorn, the sign under which he was born. The Lion may perhaps have belonged to the legions of the *triumvir* Lepidus. The Ram is the sign of the *Legio I Minervia* (raised by Domitian), and the Sun enters Aries in the month sacred to Minerva. The Twins of the *Legio II Italica* and the Archer of the *Legio II Parthica* may be similarly explained. There were excep-tions to this rule, however, for we are told that the *Legio V Alaudae* received the elephant as its symbol because of its gallant stand against the charge of Juba's elephants at Thapsus (Appian, *Bell. Civ.* ii.), and the Boar and Pegasus do not seem to have an astrological meaning. On the Column of Trajan, we see the Ram of the *Legio I Minervia* carried on a pole like that of the legionary eagle; it has been thought that the legion is thus singled out for special representation because it was commanded by Hadrian in the second Dacian War.

Under the Empire portraits of the reigning emperor (*imagines*) were also among the ensigns of the legions and carried by *imaginiferi*, who seem to have been attached to the first *cohort*. It is of these imagines that the historians speak when they tell us that on the murder of an emperor his portraits were torn down and trampled underfoot by the soldiers. Tacitus tells us that under Tiberius the effigy of Seianus 'was worshipped among the standards of the legions', and a bronze bust, now in Speier, which seems to have been one of the *imagines* carried by the legions of the Rhine, agrees in feature with a portrait head found at Pompeii under circumstances which suggest that it may represent Tiberius's favourite and *praetorian prefect*. The auxiliary *cohorts* likewise had their *signa* and *imagines*, which were similar to those of the legions.

The standard of the cavalry regiment was a *vexillum*, or flag which hung from the cross-bar of the lance. The tombstone of a soldier of the *Ala Longiniana*, a regiment recruited in Celtic districts and stationed in Lower Germany, shows such a *vexillum* decorated with the figure of a three-horned ox, which is known to have been a symbol of Gallic mythology. The several *turmae* or squadrons of the *ala* had plain *signa* with ivy-leaves hanging from the cross-bar. (Some *alae* possessed special decorations, *e.g.* the *alae torquatae*: but we have as yet no instance of the representation of such decorations on their *signa*).

The *vexillum* was also used as the standard of detachments rather than of whole corps; thus a portion of a legion detailed for special service was called a *vexillatio*, and a field force was often composed of several of these drawn from different legions; and we naturally find it as the ensign of mounted sections attached to infantry corps—the *equites legionis*, the *equites* attached to the auxiliary *cohortes equitatae*, and those belonging to each of the *praetorian cohorts*. On a relief of Marcus Aurelius which, as I believe, represents an *allocutio* delivered by the emperor in the Castra Praetoria at Rome, we see *signiferi* bearing such *vexilla*, and others carrying figures of divinities—Victoria, Mars, and Hercules. It has been suggested that Mars was the deity specially worshipped by the *speculatores*, who formed the *élite* of the Guards, and Hercules the patron of the *equites singulares*, a mounted bodyguard which existed as early as the reign of Trajan, if not before.

The *signa*, and above all the *aquila*, were objects of religious worship to the Roman soldier. The 'birthday of the eagle' was celebrated as that of the legion; the 'genius of the *signa*' is mentioned in inscriptions. We read in Livy of an oath 'by the *signa* and the eagles', and in Tacitus of a commander who saved himself from the fury of a mutinous legion by 'embracing the *signa* and the eagle and putting himself under the protection of their sanctity'. The shrine in which they were kept in camp is represented on reliefs, *e. g.* on the 'sword of Tiberius' in the British Museum, where the eagle stands between two *signa*; and its place has, as we shall see, been determined in the camps and *castella* which have been excavated. Beneath it we often find the remains of an underground chamber which served as a strong-room, containing the military chest and the savings-bank of the soldiers.

§ 3. ENGINES OF WAR.

The history of artillery in the ancient world dates from about 400 B. C., when projectile-throwing engines were used by the Syracusans (under the rule of Dionysius I) in the war with Carthage. It is true that in a list of inventions Pliny ascribes the discovery of the *catapulta* to the Cretans and that of the *ballista* to the 'Syrophoenicians'; but we do not hear of their use at any time before the war above mentioned, when they were employed with effect in the siege of Motye (397 B. C). About fifty years later they first appear in the inventories of the Athenian arsenal, and in 340 B. C. they were used in the siege of Byzantium by Philip of Macedon; this is the earliest record of their employment in Greece proper. Stone-throwing engines, as distinguished from ones which discharged arrows, are first expressly mentioned in Arrian's account of the siege of Halicarnassus by Alexander the Great.

During the Hellenistic period the use of these engines became universal; the park of artillery surrendered by Carthage to the Romans in 149 B. C. comprised 2,000 of both these. Scientific treatises were written on their construction, and the remains of these form the basis upon which our knowledge of the subject rests. The most important are the work of Philon, which is a portion of his *Handbook of Engines*, and the MSS of Heron. The date of these writers is not certain, but they probably lived at Alexandria in the second century B. C. The MSS. of Heron contain sketches of the engines described, which (allowing for errors of transmission) possess considerable value for the purposes of reconstruction.

Vitruvius describes the *catapulta* and *ballista* in two chapters of his tenth book which are based on the Alexandrian writers, and the fourth-century historian Ammianus Marcellinus gives an accurate account of the *onager*, to be described presently. The earliest representation in art of such engines is to be seen in a relief from Pergamon, now in Berlin, dating from the reign of Eumenes II (197-159 B. C). They are shown in several places on the Column of Trajan, and a relief on a tombstone in the Vatican which is described below has recently been recognised as representing a *catapulta*.

It is only within the last few years that the evidence, both literary and monumental, has been satisfactorily interpreted. For this it was necessary that technical knowledge and classical scholarship should render to each other mutual assistance; and the German writers, Rüstow and Köchly, whose work on ancient artillery held the field until recent times, fell short of the highest standard in both respects. The Greek texts were, however, critically edited by Wescher in 1867, and de Reffye, a general in the service of Napoleon III, made some advance in the construction of practical models.

The main problems were at length solved by Colonel Schramm, a German officer resident at Metz, who succeeded in constructing engines as powerful as those used by the ancients themselves. His models were exhibited before H. M. the German Emperor on June 16, 1904. His 'Euthytonon' discharged an arrow 88 cm. in length for a distance of 369.5 m., his 'Palintonon' attained a range of 184 m. with a two-pound stone projectile, and 300 m. with a one-pound leaden ball. The *onager* fired a one-pound leaden ball 140 m. These engines, together with others which will be mentioned below, are now preserved in the museum at the Saalburg. The ancient texts have meanwhile been carefully sifted and interpreted by Rudolf Schneider, and the publication of a corpus of such treatises has been commenced.

The development of ancient artillery was due to the application of a new force to the discharge of projectiles, *viz.* the elasticity of torsion produced by twisted strands of gut or horse-hair. This is entirely different from the elasticity of tension developed by the arms of a bow, which act directly upon the string and thus upon the arrow; but in order to bring it to bear, it is necessary to use a mechanical contrivance which was perhaps first applied to the cross-bow. Heron describes a weapon called the 'stomach-bow' (probably to be identified with the Roman *arcuballista*), which is a cross-bow whose stock ends in a concave cross-piece; this was pressed tightly against the body when the bow was strung.

In the centre of the stock was a hollow trough or 'pipe', and into this fitted a 'projector' of the same shape, in which the arrow was placed. By means of a series of teeth and prongs the projector could be held firmly at the point required when the bow was strung by pressure against the ground; then by withdrawing a bolt it was released and the

Tombstone of C. Vedennius Moderatus (showing *catapulta* in relief).

arrow discharged. This invention made it possible to use contrivances such as the windlass or compound pulley in order to overcome the resistance of the body whose elasticity provided the motive force. The Greek writers distinguish two kinds of engines. The first, we are told, discharged arrows, the second stones—*i. e.* the distinction is the same as that between the ones used in the siege of Byzantium. The explanation of the terms is, however, uncertain, since the descriptions of the Alexandrian writers reveal no difference in the principle of construction. It has been conjectured that the one discharged its missile point-blank, whilst the other, which was a heavier piece of ordnance, was constructed for a plunging fire. Pl XXXIX a shows a diagram of the one described by Vitruvius in side-view according to Schramm's restoration; the frame of a similar engine, as seen from the front, is shown on the relief figured on Pl. XXXVIII. This relief adorned the tombstone of C. Vedennius Moderatus, (the inscription is given by Dessau 2034), a soldier who entered the Sixteenth Legion (then quartered at Mainz) in *A. D.* 59-60, marched with it to Italy in *A. D.* 69, and fought for Vitellius; when the legion was disbanded by Vespasian, Vedennius was drafted into the Ninth Praetorian *cohort*, in which he served until his discharge in *A. D.* 77. He was retained in the service as an *evocatus Augusti*, and filled the post of *architectus armamentarii* in the Imperial arsenal.

The frame, as the relief shows, was square in outline. The side-pieces in the engine here represented (which perhaps embodied improvements invented by Vedennius), were convex in front. In the descriptions we read of a second pair of uprights, and it seems as though the strings were generally exposed to view between the uprights on either side, and the centre of the frame left open; Vedennius, however, protected his *catapulta* from the enemy's missiles by means of a shield in which only a small opening was left for the discharge of the arrow.

Near the ends of each of the cross-pieces of the frame were bored holes, through which the strands of gut or horse-hair passed. These were wound tightly round nuts both at the top and at the bottom of the frame, usually in ten layers; they are easily distinguished in the relief of Vedennius. They were made as taut as possible by means of a windlass. Through the middle of these bundles of gut passed two wooden bars which played the part of the arms of a cross-bow, but of course derived their motive power from the torsion of the strings and not from any tension of their own. The ends were connected by the 'bowstring', which discharged the arrow. (The strands seem to be

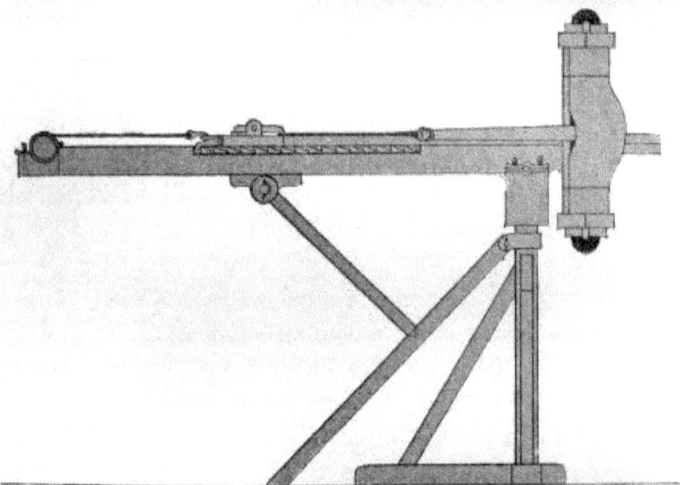

A. *Catapulta* (εὐθύτονον) restored by Schramm from Vitruvius's description.

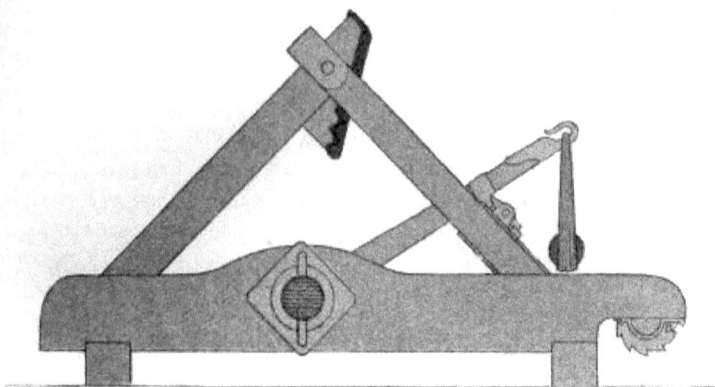

B. *Onager* (μονάγκων) restored by Schramm from Ammianus's description.

called *vincla*, the bowstring *libramentum*, in Tac. *Hist.* iii. 23). This was placed in a projector running in a groove in the 'pipe' exactly as above described.

The projector (which is shown in side-view on Pl. XXXIX a) was drawn back as far as possible by means of a strong rope worked by a handle or windlass, and fixed in its position by a catch fitting into a series of teeth. At the end of it was a 'hand' or hook, which held the bowstring, and this became stretched as the projector was drawn back, and drew the 'arms' of the catapult away from the frame, increasing the torsion of the strands. The 'hand' was held down by a bolt, which was then shot and the bowstring thus released. The catapult was supported on a pillar with stays, various forms of which are described. The heavier engines also had struts connecting the stock with the stays. As explained above, the principle of the Roman *ballista* was the same, but its construction was more solid since the projectile was heavier. (The *ballista* usually threw stones, but sometimes also wooden beams.) If it was designed for high-angle fire the pipe must have been inclined accordingly, and many modern reconstructions show the end resting on the ground.

The *onager* as described by Ammianus is represented by Pl. XXX-IX b, according to Schramm's reconstruction. Although it is not mentioned by any earlier writer (unless the term *scorpio* may sometimes include it as well as the *catapulta*) we can hardly suppose it to have been a late invention, since the principle is very simple. The strings were stretched, not vertically as in the *catapulta* and *ballista*, but horizontally; the ends are seen in the centre of the carriage in our illustration. The single arm ended in a hook, from which hung a sling containing the projectile. It was drawn back by means of a rope wound round an axle at the back of the carriage, and secured in its horizontal position by a bolt, the release of which caused it to spring back to an almost vertical position, where it was checked by a pad, the missile being meanwhile discharged by the sling. The recoil was violent, and the *onager* (which took its name from the wild ass because of its powerful 'kick') was therefore placed on a turf platform in action.

The three engines already described were the only ones in regular use in the Roman Army. Others are described by the Greek writers on mechanics, but it is doubtful whether they were more than ingenious toys. Such were Ctesibius' (the teacher of Philon), in which compressed air was used to force the arms into position, and that of his pupil, with elastic steel plates in place of the strands of gut. Philon was also the inventor of a device for tightening the strings by means of wedges. He describes a machine gun or *mitrailleuse*, invented by one Dionysius of Alexandria, which fired a succession of arrows supplied by a magazine or hopper placed above.

The Romans employed guns mounted on a carriage (*carroballistae*), which was drawn into action by a team of horses or mules. (Vegetius tells us that such artillery was posted in rear of the heavy infantry in action). Such a gun is shown on the Column of Trajan, from which Fig. 41 a is taken. It will be seen that the projecting parts of the strings are not visible, as on the tombstone of Vedennius, but are protected by caps. The projector contained an arrow. The gunners wear the ordinary costume of legionaries; and there is in fact no evidence to show that the Roman artillery was served by a special corps of trained men. The historians and military writers, on the contrary, imply that any legionary was competent to handle the guns.

Fig. 41 a.

The use of engines in siege-warfare was chiefly for defensive purposes. The projectiles which they hurled would not have sufficed to make a breach in solidly constructed walls, although doubtless an artillery preparation was effective in clearing the battlements of their defenders before an attempt was made to scale them with ladders. The calibre of the *catapulta* was determined by the length of the arrow, which varied from 3 spans, *i.e.* 27 inches, to 3 ells, *i.e.* 4½ feet. The effective range of the largest of these engines would be about 1,000–1,200 feet. The calibre of the *ballista* was fixed by the weight of the projectile estimated in *minae*; this varied in practice from 10 *minae* to 60 (or 1 *talent* = about 53 lb.). This was the heaviest ordnance in general use: the *ballista* of three-talent calibre, constructed (according to Athenaeus) by Archimedes, and those constructed by the Massaliots during Caesar's siege of their town, which hurled twelve-foot beams, were quite exceptional. The technical writers give a scheme of proportions for the construction of these engines. The *modulus* was the diameter of the opening through which the strings passed. In the *catapulta* this was one-ninth of the length of the arrow. For the *ballista* a more elaborate formula was used. The weight of the projectile (in *drachms*) was multiplied by 100, and the cube root of this quantity + one-tenth gave the diameter in *dactyls* (threequarters of an inch).

It has been said that projectile-throwing engines were not of primary use in siege operations except for defence. For attack their place was taken by others, the object of which was either to make a breach in the enemy's walls or to protect sappers engaged in undermining them. Such engines and devices had been used from early times in Oriental warfare, (they are represented in Assyrian sculptures, and the invention of the ram is ascribed by ancient writers to the Phoenicians), and had been carried to a high degree of perfection by the Hellenistic Greeks. They are described by the writers mentioned at the beginning of this section, as well as by Aeneas Tacticus, an author of the fourth century B. C.

The principal engine of attack was the battering-ram (*aries*), a huge beam (we hear of such 60, 80, and 120 feet in length), with an iron head, the form of which gave its name to the machine; it is clearly shown on the Column of Trajan and the Arch of Septimius Severus. In its simplest form the ram was carried by a file of soldiers and impelled by the force of their arms; thus, on Trajan's Column we see Dacians using it against a Roman fort. The next step was to suspend it by rings from a stout pole and to swing it against the wall by means of ropes. But both methods were superseded in general use by the frame on wheels, in which the ram, suspended from a horizontal beam, was moved up to the walls. The frame was called the 'tortoise' (*testudo*), and had a wooden roof covered with clay or hides as a protection against fire. (To be distinguished from the *testudo* formed by the locked shields of a body of men advancing to the attack on a fortified place; the *scuta* formed a solid roof which no missiles could penetrate).

The more elaborate had several stories, in order to play upon the wall at the most suitable height; on the Arch of Severus we see soldiers mounting to the second story of such an engine. A variety of the ram was the 'borer' (*terebra*) described by Vitruvius, which had a sharp point and was used to make holes in a wall. The *falx muralis*, or 'sickle', attached to the end of a swinging beam, loosened the stones on the top of the wall. Movable towers (*turres*) moving on wheels were used in assaulting fortified towers; the Greeks gave the name 'city-taker' to the largest of these, such as those of several stories carrying artillery on their platforms which were used by Demetrius Poliorketes at the siege of Rhodes. Caesar describes the construction of a large tower of this kind by his troops when besieging Massilia in B. C. 49, and Josephus tells us that they were used in the siege of Jerusalem (*A. D.* 70).

For the protection of troops engaged in sapping and mining the *musculus, vinea* and *pluteus* were used. In the account of the siege of Massilia already quoted Caesar describes the *musculus* at length. It was a wooden shed 60 feet long, 4 feet wide, and 5 feet high, with a sloping roof covered first with bricks and earth, then with hides, and over these with wet mattresses as a protection against fire. This covered gallery was moved up against the wall on rollers, and the foundations were then sapped with crowbars. The *vinea* differed from the *musculus* in having one of the longer sides open; the *pluteus* was a small screen, usually of wickerwork, for the protection of small bodies of men.

§ 4. TROPHIES.

It was the custom of the Greeks, when victorious in battle, to mark the spot where the rout of the enemy began; a tree trunk was felled, and adorned with armour stripped from the fallen foe. The Macedonian kings did not observe this custom, nor was it the practice of the Romans in early times; the spoils of the enemy were used to decorate public buildings in Rome. In the later Republic, however, they adopted the Greek custom. We hear that Cn. Domitius Ahenobarbus and Q. Fabius Maximus, after defeating the Allobroges in 121 B.C, set up permanent trophies (described as 'towers of white stone', *i.e.* marble) at the confluence of the Rhone and Isère; Pausanias saw two trophies erected by Sulla on the scene of his defeat of Archelaus, the general of Mithridates in 86 B. C.; and a few years later Pompey, at the close of the Sertorian war in Spain, set up a monument at the crossing of the Pyrenees with an inscription commemorating his reduction of 876 towns or villages.

No remains of these trophies exist; but at La Turbie, overlooking Monaco, may be seen the ruins of a fortress, the core of which is formed by the Tropaeum Alpium, a monument set up in 16 B.C. to commemorate the subjugation of the Alpine tribes. The inscription, giving the names of forty-six peoples, is preserved by Pliny the elder, and small fragments of the original have been discovered. The ancient aspect of the monument can be recovered from the descriptions written in the sixteenth century, when it was still in a fair state of preservation. Upon a shallow plinth stood a massive square substructure with two doors and staircases by which the ascent was made to the circular tower, surrounded by a colonnade in two stories, adorned with pilasters (between which, in the lower story, were niches for statues) and crowned with a cupola supporting the trophy proper—described by the mediaeval writers as a 'statue of Augustus', from its resemblance to an armed figure. In Rome itself we have the so-called 'trophies of Marius', which now adorn the balustrade of the Capitoline piazza; they were brought thither from a monumental fountain on the Esquiline, and probably commemorated Domitian's victories on the Rhine and Danube. The usual type of the *tropaeum* is here amplified by the addition of the figure of a captive at the foot of the tree trunk.

But the most remarkable monument of this kind is the 'Trophy of Trajan' at Adam-Klissi in the Dobrudja, reproduced on PL. XL after the reconstruction published by Furtwängler, which is more accurate than that given in the work of Benndorf mentioned below. A flight of steps was surmounted by a circular base, the upper portion of which was decorated with a series of panels divided by pilasters and carved in relief with representations of Romans and barbarians on the march or in action, and crowned with a cornice and embattled parapet, the crenellations being adorned with reliefs of barbarian prisoners. The base has a sloping roof surmounted by a hexagonal structure in two storeys: on one face of the upper storey was the inscription which recorded the erection of the trophy by Trajan, and above was a frieze representing pieces of armour. The trophy proper crowned the edifice, the height of which was equal to the diameter of the base (including the steps).

An acute controversy has been waged as to the date of the monument and its reliefs. The fragments of the inscription leave no doubt that it was dedicated by Trajan to Mars Ultor; and the adjacent town was called Tropaeum Trajani. Hard by is a monument erected in memory of 8,000 Roman soldiers who fell on this spot; and it is reasonable to suppose that a disaster took place here under Domitian, which was avenged by Trajan and commemorated by the trophy. Furtwängler, however, maintained that though Trajan restored the monument and gave his name to it, it was originally set up by M. Licinius Crassus

Trophy of Adam-Klissi (restored by Furtwängler).

(grandson of the *triumvir*), at the time of his expedition against the Bastarnae in 29 B. C, but was left without an inscription, since Crassus was acting as the *legatus* of Augustus. The style of the reliefs is very rude, and betrays the hand of the legionary; but there are details (especially in the ornament) which seem to point to the time of Trajan rather than that of Augustus.

§ 5. CAMPS.

Nothing in the public life of the Romans bears such eloquent testimony to the orderly and practical spirit which gave them the mastery of the ancient world than their scientific method of encampment. A Roman Army on the march never bivouacked without constructing an entrenched camp (*castra*) large enough to contain the whole force, together with beasts and baggage; and the marching kit of the Roman soldier included a number of stakes—sometimes as many as seven—for use in forming the palisade with which the earthen mound (*vallum*) surrounding the camp was strengthened. In protracted campaigns, and in the occupation of conquered territory, permanent camps (*castra stativa*) became necessary; in summer the troops were kept under canvas in *c. aestiva*, but for winter quarters (*c. hiberna*) barracks were built whose remains have been preserved in many parts of the Empire. These we are enabled to interpret by means of the descriptions of ancient writers.

On the one hand, we find in the sixth book of Polybius a full account of the planning of a camp designed for a consular army of two legions with its complement of auxiliaries; on the other, we possess in the tract *de munitionibus castrorum*, which passes for a work of the land-surveyor Hyginus, but appears to belong to the early third century *A. D.*, a description of the summer camp of an army of three legions with auxiliary contingents planned according to the regulations of the later Empire. These documents, together with some other passages in ancient literature, (especially Josephus, *Bell.Iud.* iii. 5, written about *A. D.* 75), when read in the light of extant remains, enable us to trace in some measure the history of Roman camp-making.

The planning of camps (*metatio castrorum*) was a department of the land-surveyor's art. The *groma* was used in orientation; the divisions of the camp were formed by *kardines* (meridian lines) and *decumani* (*base lines*); the quarters of the troops were disposed *per scamna et strigas* (parallel lines to the *kardines* and *decumani*). In theory the camp was held to face eastwards, and the *decumanus* was accordingly the road connecting the *porta praetoria*—the 'commander's entrance' by which the army issued from the camp—with the *porta decumana* in the rear, while the *kardo* traversed the camp from north to south under the name of the *via principalis*, connecting the *porta principalis sinistra* with the *p. p. dextra*. But it need scarcely be said that in practice the orientation of the camp was determined by military considerations, and the terms of art were used in a purely conventional sense.

The scheme of Polybius (cf. Fig. 42, after Nissen) provides, as was said above, for an army of two legions, each numbering 4,500 men (1,200 *hastati* + 1,200 *principes* + 600 *triarii* + 1,200 *velites* + 300 *equites*), together with the allied contingents (normally 4,200 foot + 600 horse to each legion), a certain number of *auxilia, i.e.* mercenary troops, and a special corps of allies called *extraordinarii*, numbering 2,100 foot + 600 horse; from these last the bodyguard of the commander was selected. The principle which governs the distribution of these forces is that the *pars postica*, in the land-surveyor's sense of the word, is assigned to the headquarters, the staff and the *extraordinarii*; while the *pars antica* contains the legions in the centre, the allies at the sides of the camp. The *pars postica* stands to the *pars antica* in the proportion of 3:2. The system of measurement is decimal and the unit 50 feet =10 paces =1 *vorsus*.

The first act of the *metator* was to plant a white flag in the spot which was to be occupied by the commander's tent, which occupied the centre of a square of 200 feet, known as the *praetorium*; in the corners of this were the *tribunal*, from which the general harangued his troops, and the *auguratorium*, where he took the auspices before marching out to battle. Before the *praetorium* stood an altar; and a line parallel with its front, and 50 feet distant therefrom marked the position of the *principia, i.e.* the quarters of the officers, *viz.* the twelve *tribunes* attached to the two legions, the *praefecti* in command of the allied troops, and the *legati* belonging to the general's staff. Along the front of the *principia* ran the *via principalis*, which took its name from them: this was 100 feet wide.

In the forepart of the camp a legion, together with its complement (*ala*) of allies, was quartered on either side of the *via praetoria*, which led from the *praetorium* to the front gate (*porta praetoria*); this road, as well as the *via quintana*, which intersected it at right angles and divided the quarters of the legion in half, was 50 feet broad. The tents were disposed in *strigae*, six on either side of the *via praetoria,* each 500 feet in length, divided from each other by roads 50 feet broad. The

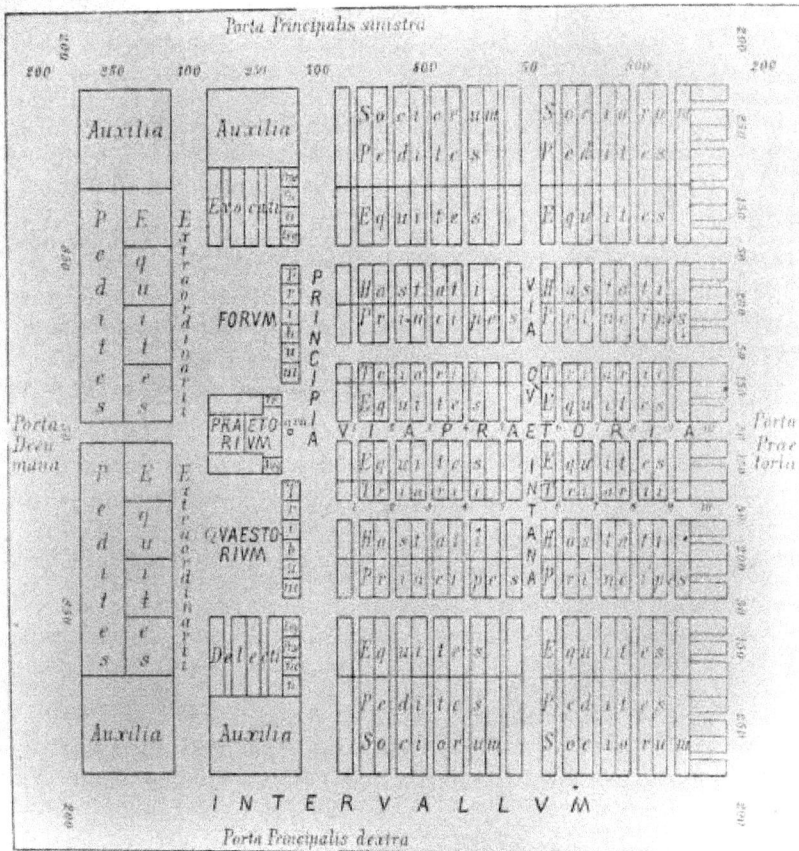

Porta Principalis sinistra

200 250 100 250 100 800 50 800 200

Auxilia Auxilia Sociorum Sociorum
Pedites Pedites

Extraordinarii Equites Equites

P. E Hastati Hastati
e q Principes VIA Principes
d u
i i FORVM Eq[u]ites O[?] Equites
t t PRINCIPIA V[?]
e e
s s PRAETORIVM VIA·P·RAET·O·RIA
Equites Equites
Triarii Triarii

P. E Hastati Hastati
e q QVAESTORIVM Principes Principes
d u
i i
t t Equites Equites
e e
s s Pedites Pedites
Auxilia Auxilia Sociorum Sociorum

INTERVALLVM

Porta Principalis dextra

Fig. 42. The camp according to Polybius (from Nissen).

striga adjoining the *via praetoria* was occupied by the legionary cavalry, whose quarters were 100 feet deep, and the *triarii*, to whom 50 feet were allowed. In the next *striga* were the *hastati* and *principes*, who divided the breadth of 200 feet equally: finally came the *striga* assigned to the allies, divided between foot and horse (the latter inside) in the proportion of 250: 150 feet.

So far, the description of Polybius is quite clear: the breadth of the camp, it will be observed, works out at 1,750 feet, and as an open space of 200 feet (*intervallum*) was left between the tents and the earthworks, the total comes to 2,150 feet. The arrangements of the *pars postica* are not so clearly described. Here the space was divided *per scamna*, not *per strigas*. The *scamnum* assigned to the officers was 50 feet in depth; in breadth it was no doubt equal to the frontage of the *strigae*, so that the tribunes were lodged opposite to the legionaries and the *praefecti* (and probably also the *legati*) opposite to the *socii* whom they commanded. Behind this *scamnum*, in the spaces 200 feet deep to the right and left of the *praetorium*, were the forum, where the market of the camp was held and booty put up to auction, and on the other side the *quaestorium*, where the *quaestor*, or paymaster, and other departmental officials transacted their business. On the extreme right and left were encamped the bodyguard. Behind this division of the camp ran a road 100 feet broad, and finally a *scamnum* 250 feet deep, cut in two by the road (50 feet wide) leading to the *porta decumana*. Here were quartered the extraordinary, the infantry, as usual, being on the outside, while the barbarian *auxilia* were posted at the ends of the *scamnum*. It will be seen that the camp thus formed a perfect square.

The description of Polybius leaves us without precise information on various points of detail, notably as to the position assigned to the *velites*, of whom we learn that they 'manned the outer front of the camp': this has been held to mean that they bivouacked outside the camp; but it may be that part of them at least served as pickets on the *intervallum*. If they were drawn in equal strength from legionaries and *socii*, they must have numbered 4,800. Having thus described the camp, Polybius adds that when two consular armies, each of two legions, were encamped within a rampart, the *extraordinarii* of each army were posted side by side in the centre, so that the two armies were back to back; but when they encamped separately, 'the *forum*, *quaestorium*, and *praetorium* were placed between the two legions.

Now there are several passages in Livy—all of which refer to wars earlier than the time when Polybius wrote his history—which imply the disposition here indicated; it may be represented by the annexed figure (Fig. 43). We hear of the *porta decumana*, evidently the same as the *porta quaestoria* of other passages, by which the enemy enter and capture the *quaestorium*; again, a consul places *cohortes extraordinariae* at the *porta praetoria*, legions at the *portae principales*, and an *ala sociorum* at the *porta quaestoria*. Moreover, in the order of march the *extraordinarii* formed the vanguard, and it is reasonable to suppose that the order of march was followed as nearly as possible in the order of encampment. Lastly, the camps of the Empire, as we shall see, are based on the same scheme; and it seems best to conclude that the camp traced in detail by Polybius is really a modification of the normal arrangement adopted when two armies operated in conjunction.

We find the same disposition of parts in the description of the so-called Hyginus, to which we must now turn (cf. Fig. 44). The date of, the work is uncertain, but as the *equites legionis* have ceased to exist, it can scarcely be earlier than the third century *A. D.* The expeditionary force which Hyginus has in view consists of three legions and a number of auxiliary regiments, both regular and irregular (included under the term *supplementa*). The presence of a camel-corps seems to show that the scene of the expedition is laid in the East. The *groma* marked the centre of the *via principalis*, which, together with the *via quintana*, divided the camp into three main portions. Between the *porta praetoria* and the *via principalis* lay the *praetentura*; on the other side of the *via principalis* was the *praetorium*, from which the central part of the camp took the name of *latera praetorii*; beyond the *via quintana* was the *retentura*. Hyginus lays it down as a rule that the camp is, as far as possible, to be divided into three *equal* parts; but the measurements which he gives allow somewhat less depth to the *retentura* than to the other sections.

The legionary force was quartered in a series of *strigae* and *scamna* running round the whole encampment, and separated from it by a road called the *via sagularis*. (If the reading of the MSS. is right, *sagularis* must be connected with *sagum;* in fig 39 the slinger is using his *sagum* to hold his missiles; *angularis* has been suggested as a correction). No legionaries were found inside of this line except the first *cohorts* of the First and Second Legions, which were posted on the outside of the *latera praetorii*, and the first four *cohorts* of the Third Legion, which were in the *praetentura*. In this section we find two *scamna* immediately adjoining the *via principalis* assigned to the *legati* and *tribuni*; behind them come four large cavalry regiments (*alae miliariae*), and then

125

some light horse (Moorish and Pannonian) and marines detached for service from the fleets at Misenum and Ravenna. With the four *cohorts* mentioned above, this exhausts the list of troops quartered in the *praetentura*, where we also find the armoury (*fabrica*) and hospitals (*valetudinarium* and *veterinarium*).

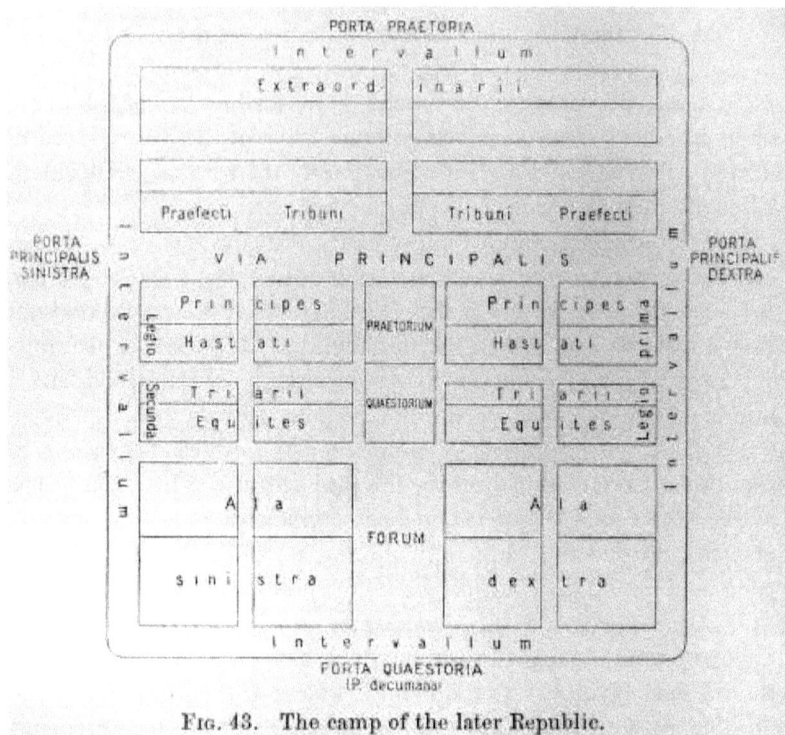

Fig. 43. The camp of the later Republic.

The divisions are *per scamna*, not *per strigas*, as in the other sections. In the *scamnum* of the *legati*, on the *via principalis*, room was found for the *scholae*, or club-rooms, of the three legions.

The *praetorium* was oblong in shape, and extended from the *via principalis* to the *via quintana*. On either side were the quarters of the commander's staff, next to which came the guards (*cohortes praetoriae*) with their complement of mounted men (*equites praetoriani* and *e. singulares*). The remaining space was filled by cavalry regiments (*alae quingenariae*) and the privileged *cohorts* mentioned above. Finally, we come to the *retentura*, the centre of which was filled in its whole length by the *quaestorium*; this, as Hyginus is careful to explain, was no longer occupied by the *quaestor* (who had long ceased to accompany the

126

magistrate on active service), but served for prisoners, hostages, and booty. To right and left of it were quartered the auxiliary *cohorts* and the various irregular corps of barbarian origin—Cantabrians, Britons, Palmyrenes, Gaetulians, and Dacians.

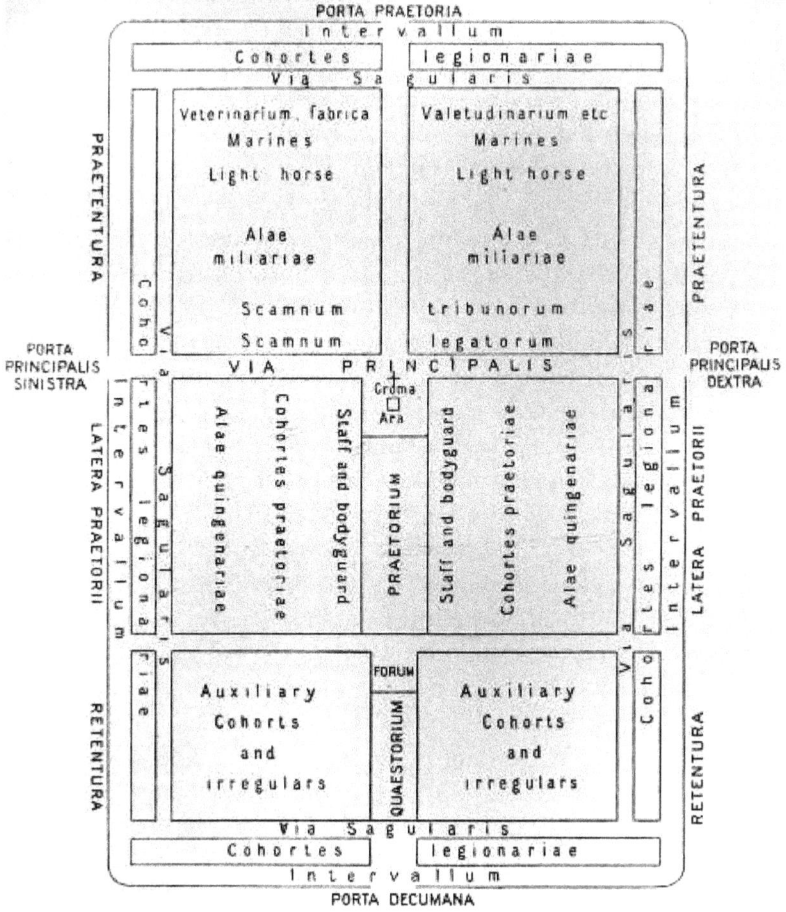

FIG. 44. The camp described by Hyginus.

Beside the changes noted above, and those which will be obvious from the foregoing description, it is to be observed that the measurements given by Hyginus are based on a duodecimal system. The length of the *praetorium*, for example, is fixed at 720 feet, and that of the *quaestorium* at 480. Again, in calculating the *pedatura*, or space measured in feet allotted to each contingent, the unit is the *striga* of 60 feet in breadth and 120 feet in length, which was assigned to the legionary *maniple* of two *centuries*. (The scheme of the *striga* is shown in Fig. 46). Moreover, there is a notable contraction in the space allotted to each soldier. Polybius allows 10,000 square feet for the *maniple* of 120 men, Hyginus 7,200 square feet for the maniple of 160; and Polybius assigns to the *turma* of 30 horsemen a space equal to the *maniple*, while in Hyginus's time the *striga* has to accommodate two *turmae*, each of 40 men.

The legionary camps of the Empire are becoming known to us with ever-increasing distinctness through the excavations of the past twenty-five years. The most important of these have taken place (*a*) at Carnuntum (Petronell on the Danube, in Lower Austria), a post garrisoned at least as early as the reign of Claudius by the *Legio XV Apollinaris*, which, as is proved by a fragmentary inscription, built a permanent camp there in *A. D.* 73, after its return from the Eastern frontier; (*b*) at Lambaesis (Lambèse) in Numidia, which from the reign of Trajan onwards was the headquarters of the *Legio III Augusta*—the permanent camp seems to have been built under Hadrian; (*c*) at Novaesium (Neuss) on the Lower Rhine, which, as the results of the excavation have been fully published, will here be described as typical.

Of the four legions which constituted the Lower German army corps, two were originally stationed by Augustus at Cologne; these were the First and the Twentieth (*Valeria Victrix*). Under Tiberius, as it would seem, this force was split up; the First Legion was transferred to Bonna (Bonn), the Twentieth went north to Novaesium, a site whence it could not only keep watch against the German tribes on the right bank of the Rhine, but also maintain communications with the authorities in Belgic Gaul by the valley of the Erft, which here falls into the Rhine. In *A. D.* 43 the Twentieth Legion went to Britain as part of Claudius's expeditionary force, and there remained; its place was taken by the *Legio XVI Gallica*, hitherto quartered at Mainz.

It was apparently this legion which built the first stone camp on the site; its arrangements prove that it was designed to shelter not merely the legion itself, but also two auxiliary *cohorts* and a cavalry regiment (*ala*). In the revolt of Civilis (*A. D.* 69-70) the soldiers of the Sixteenth Legion mutinied once and again, murdering first Hordeonius Flaccus, the aged and incapable *Legatus* of Lower Germany, and then Dillius Vocula, the gallant commander of the Twenty-Second Legion; the camp then fell into the hands of the rebels and was partly destroyed, but was rebuilt in *A. D.* 70 by Petillius Cerialis after the suppression of the revolt. The Sixteenth Legion was disbanded by Vespasian, and its place was taken by the *Legio VI Victrix,* which had come from Spain.

This legion formed the garrison of Novaesium until the early years of the second century *A. D.* It appears to have taken part in the first Dacian War of Trajan (*A. D.* 101-2), and if it returned to Novaesium its stay there was of brief duration, for in *A. D.* 105 it was transferred to Castra Vetera (Xanten) to replace the Tenth Legion, which was summoned by Trajan to take part in the second Dacian War. Henceforward the camp was only occupied by detachments, and fell into disrepair; about *A. D.* 250, under Gallienus, a small fort, capable of holding an *ala,* was constructed in the centre of the deserted space, but was only held for a short time. In the last quarter of the third century the civil settlement from which the modern Neuss is descended, which had sprung up at some distance from the old camp,

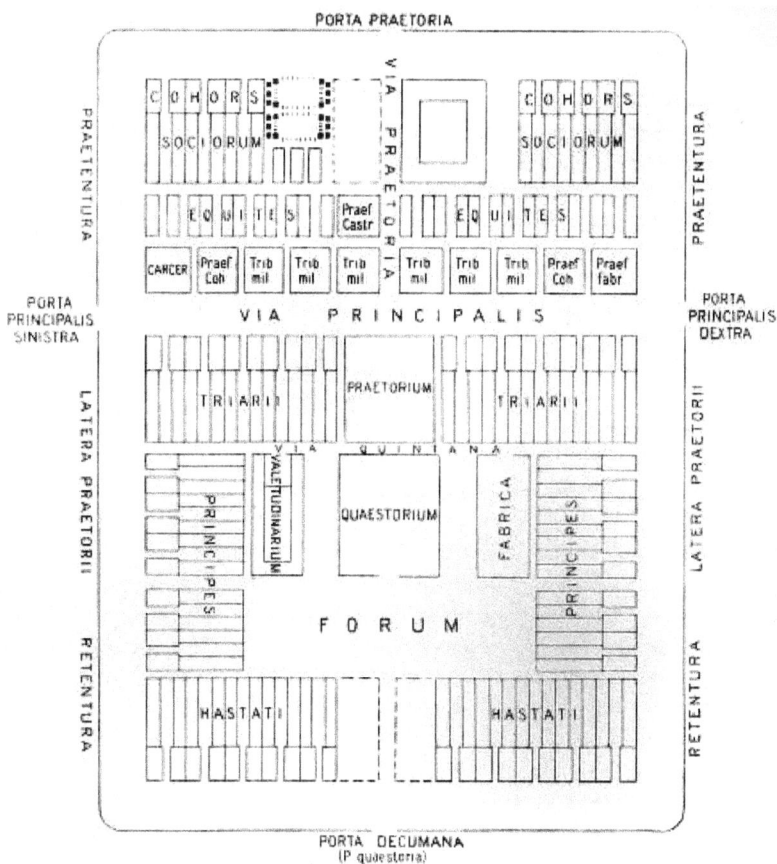

FIG. 45.   The camp at Novaesium before A. D. 70, according to Oxé.

was surrounded with walls and became the centre of defence in the district; we read that the Emperor Julian repaired its fortifications in *A. D.* 359-60.

The remains found at Novaesium belong in part to the camp built under Claudius, in part to the restoration of *A. D.* 70, and it was no easy task to determine the arrangements of the earlier structure. Nevertheless, it has been found possible to trace a fairly trustworthy plan of the camp as it existed before the revolt of the Rhine, taking the descriptions of Polybius and Hyginus as a guide. Fig. 45 is based on the results of Nissen's researches, published in the *Bonner Jahrbücher* for 1904, but is somewhat simplified and incorporates the suggestions of Oxé as to the distribution of the troops.

The camp encloses a space of 24.70 ha., a little less than the sister-camp of Bonn, which covers about 25 ha. This may be taken to be the normal size of the camps built under the Julio-Claudian dynasty, when legions and *auxilia* lived within the same walls. The Flavian camp of Carnuntum was only about three-fifths as large; this is because Vespasian, taught by the experience of Civilis's revolt, assigned separate stations to the legionary and allied troops. The camp of Lambaesis, which likewise contained a legion only, is much larger, about 21 ha.; but the growing luxury of the service accounts for this. Finally, the new regulations of Septimius Severus, which permitted the legionary to live with his wife and children, put an end to camp life and with it to the old Roman discipline; hence the area of the camp which he caused to be built at Albano for the second Parthian Legion—the first to be permanently quartered in Italy—is smaller even than that of Carnuntum in area.

Whilst the camp at Bonn was square, that of Novaesium, in accordance with the prescriptions of the later authorities, was of rectangular outline. Taking the outer edge of the ditch as the line of measurement, its sides are respectively about 2,000 and 1,540 Roman feet in length; the proportion is nearly that of 3:4 instead of the 2:3 prescribed by Hyginus. Within the area thus marked out we find first a ditch which was originally 40 feet in width, then a solid wall 4 to 5 feet thick, and within this an embankment of earth (*vallum*) which in the original camp was 10 feet wide, but after the restoration of *A. D.* 70 was extended to a breadth of 30 feet, and this was gradually increased to 40 feet. The total space between the wall and the camp-buildings—the *intervallum* of Roman writers—was 100 feet, and of this, 20 feet was occupied by a road—the *via sagularis* or *angularis* of Hyginus—running along the buildings, so that the free space surrounding the camp was reduced to 40 feet by the gradual extension of the *vallum*.

The wall was pierced by four gates; the *porta praetoria*, which faced the Rhine, was 100 feet wide, the others somewhat narrower. The *via principalis*, 125 feet wide, divides the camp into two unequal portions, roughly in the proportion of 3:5. The smaller of these is the *praetentura* of Hyginus, and is divided into two halves by the *via praetoria* which leads directly to the *praetorium*. The barracks of the legions and *auxilia* are clearly traceable, and correspond closely enough with the description of Hyginus, which, it is to be remembered, applies to the camp of an army on the march.

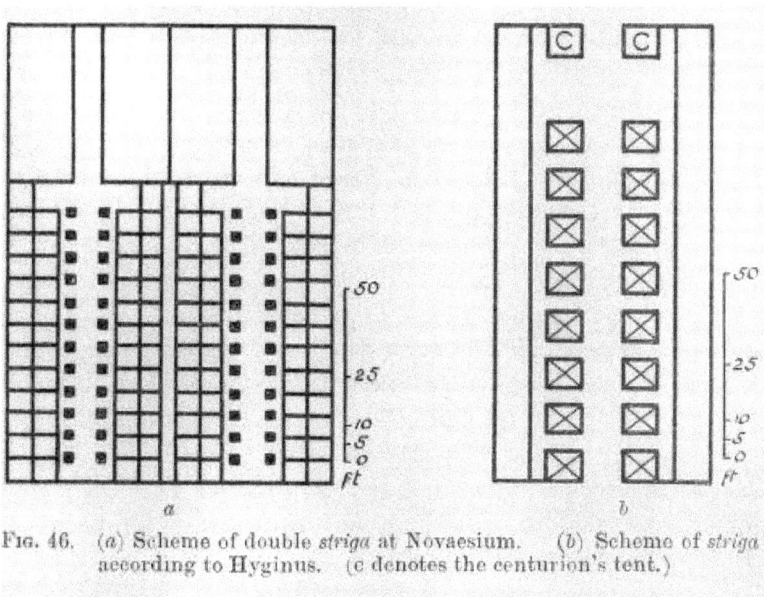

FIG. 46. (a) Scheme of double *striga* at Novaesium. (b) Scheme of *striga* according to Hyginus. (c denotes the centurion's tent.)

He tells us that to each *manipulus*, formed by two *centuriae* of 80 men, a *striga* of 120 x 60 feet was assigned. In the centre was an open lane (*via*) 12 feet broad, and on either side were ranged the tents of the *centuria*. Each of these was 10 feet square, and gave shelter to a *contubernium* of eight men. They were separated by an interval of 2 feet (*incrementum tensurae*), and as a certain proportion of the *centuria* was always on guard during the night, only eight tents were set up for the privates beside one for the centurion. Behind the tents a space 5 feet wide was reserved for arms and accoutrements, and behind this again 9 feet were set apart for the sumpter beasts (*iumenta*): thus, the quarters assigned to the *manipulus*—the *striga*, divided into two *hemistrigia* for the *centuriae*—may be represented by Fig. 46 (*b*); and will be seen at once that it corresponds closely enough with the typical *striga* at Novaesium represented by Fig. 46 (*a*).

In a permanent camp more space was naturally allowed; hence we find that the *strigae* at Novaesium measure on the average 100 x 250 feet. At one end of the *striga* we find a residence occupying one-third of its length, which was clearly intended for the *centurion* and his assistants, the *optio*, *tesserarius*, and *signifer*. The room next to this was probably used by the sentries, and the remainder of the space was occupied by the *contubernia*. This part of the *striga* was diminished in breadth by 6 feet in order that an open space for roof drainage might be left between the *strigae*, which were built back to back.

The central roadway accounted for one-sixth of the 100 feet of frontage; it was flanked by open sheds whose position is marked by lines of posts which, we may suppose, supported a pent-house roof; under these sheds the beasts of burden were doubtless tethered. The *contubernium* itself had two rooms, of which the outer, where the arms were kept, was 8 and a third feet, and the inner, where the soldiers slept, was 15 feet deep; the breadth of each *contubernium* was 12 feet. The remaining space is accounted for by the walls, which were some-what less than 2 feet in thickness. As the restored plan, Fig. 45, shows, such barracks were originally constructed both on the north front and on all sides of the space south of the *via principalis*, corresponding with the *latera praetorii* and *retentura* of Hyginus, except for the space oc-cupied by the *praetorium*. (This plan is in parts conjectural, since great changes were made in the camp-buildings after *A. D.* 70. Doubtful points are noted in the text). These latter by themselves furnished suf-ficient accommodation for the legion.

The distribution of the tactical units is, however, a matter of con-jecture. Nissen arranges the ten *cohorts* as follows: the first and second in the place of honour on either side of the *praetorium*, the third to the sixth on the eastern and western sides, and the remaining four on the south front. Oxé (whose arrangement is followed in Fig. 45) thinks that the order of the maniples occupying the several *strigae* cor-responded with the grade of seniority of their *centurions*—the *hastati* being on the south front, the *principes* on the two sides, and the *triarii* flanking the *praetorium*. If there was a sudden call to arms, the *triplex acies* was thus naturally formed as the troops left the camp without complicated evolutions. The infantry quarters on the north front must have been occupied by auxiliary troops, probably two *cohortes miliariae* of 1,000 men each.

The quarters of the cavalry are no less easy to recognise. To begin with, immediately to the south of the quarters assigned to the auxiliary *cohorts* we find a row of buildings whose destination is clearly indicated by the finds of harness, &c, made therein. Here the breadth of the *striga* is from 80 to 90 feet; the roadway is 18 feet broad, and the *contubernia*, like those of the infantry, have an outer and inner chamber, 14 and 16 feet deep; the former of these must be the stall. The length of the *striga* is about 116 feet, and is divided into nine *contubernia* which (allowing for the thickness of the walls) are rather less than 12 feet broad. Since the number of *strigae* originally allowed, no less than the nature of the cavalry force to be accommodated, is a matter of doubt, we cannot be sure how many troopers found a place in each *contubernium*.

It is held by Nissen that an *ala quingenaria* numbering 480 horsemen was quartered in this part of the camp; but we have also to account for the mounted troops attached to the legion, consisting in a force of 120 horsemen—the *equites legionis*—in four squadrons (*turmae*). (The only inscription found at Novaesium which mentions the Sixteenth Legion (see above) is that on the tombstone of one of these *equites*). As this force had ceased to exist in the time of Hyginus, his description gives no clue to the place which they occupied; but in Polybius's camp, as we saw, the legionary cavalry had their quarters in a central position; and Nissen believes that at Novaesium two squadrons found a place in two *strigae* on either side of the *praetorium*. Later alterations have, however, made it impossible to determine this question.

Immediately to the north of the *via principalis* were the *principia*. What we here find is a row of detached buildings which were in great part destroyed when the third-century fort mentioned above was built. It is clear, however, that there were five such buildings to the west of the *via praetoria*, and, since the original camp was built on strictly symmetrical lines, we may assume that there were once a like number to the east.

★★★★★★

A *schola* took the place of the two easternmost houses after *A. D.* 70. A *schola*, or 'lounge,' is often found in public places, such as the fora of Roman towns, as at Simitthus (Chemtou) in North Africa; they are usually semi-circular in form, with a bench running round the wall. From this the apsidal termination of some of the *scholae* at Lambaesis is derived.

133

★★★★★★

The westernmost building is quite different in plan from the others, and was certainly a prison (*carcer*); it contained fifty-eight cells measuring 4 feet by something less than 6. The others, whose measurements average roughly 125 feet square, conform (as is shown by the best-preserved example, next to the *carcer*) to the type of the Roman dwelling-house. They were without doubt the residences of the officers, and if there were originally nine such available, we may assign them to the six tribunes of the legion, the *praefects* of the two *auxiliary cohorts*, and the *praefect* of the *ala*.

Finally, we come to the group of buildings which occupies the centre of the camp. We saw that in the scheme of Hyginus the central position is filled by the *praetorium*, or headquarters building; behind this, and separated from it by the *via quintana*, was the *quaestorium*. Both these buildings are easily identified at Novaesium, although their original outlines are obscured by reconstruction. The *praetorium* in its original shape was 250 feet square; in its centre was a courtyard 150 feet square, surrounded by a roofed passage, upon which opened the living-rooms and offices, about thirty in number. It was separated by a road 25 feet wide from the *quaestorium*, a building measuring 250 x 300 feet, whose original plan can no longer be traced owing to changes presently to be described.

On either side of the *quaestorium* were buildings 300 feet in length, symmetrically disposed. There can be no doubt that that which lay to the west was the camp-hospital, for several surgical instruments were found in its remains. It was entered from the north, and in its central portion was planned on the lines of a dwelling-house. This structure was separated by a passage 20 feet wide from an outer rectangle consisting in a number of small suites of rooms suitable for the isolation of patients undergoing medical treatment. The corresponding building to the east of the *quaestorium*, which contains some remains of wall-painting in fresco, but was almost entirely destroyed when the third-century fort was built, is hard to identify.

Nissen conjectures that the armoury, workshops, &c. (*fabrica*), are to be placed here; in that case the frescoed rooms will belong to the quarters of the *praefectus fabrum*; but, as we shall see, the *fabrica* seems to have been elsewhere, and it seems possible that the *praefectus castrorum* had his residence in this building. Behind the *quaestorium* we find, to the east of the *via decumana*, a space in which few traces of buildings remain, measuring 200 x 350. This must be the *forum*; and in the corresponding position to the west of the road we find workshops, clearly belonging to the *fabrica*.

Such in its main outlines was the camp of Novaesium under the Julio-Claudian emperors. It is clear that it resembles the camp of Polybius—when allowance has been made for the change in the position of the *quaestorium* and in the proportions of the two sections of the camp—far more closely than that of Hyginus. The measurements are on the same decimal system. The position assigned to the auxiliaries on the north front corresponds with that of the *socii extraordinarii* under the Republic. The flanks of the legion, it is true, are not covered by allied troops; but it is to be remembered that the legion of the Empire, with its 6,000 combatants, was practically equivalent, not to the legion of the Republic—3,000 heavy-armed + 1,200 light-armed troops— but to that unit with its complement of allies. Certain changes are due to the fact that we are dealing with the permanent cantonments of a standing army; the hospital and workshops, for example, are obvious additions. The spaces allotted to the soldiers' quarters, too, are greater than those given by Polybius; *e. g.* the *maniple* has 25,000 square feet instead of 10,000. But it should be borne in mind that one-third of this space is set apart for the *centurion* and non-commissioned officers—a visible token of the hierarchical system which Augustus introduced into the army as elsewhere.

In the period following the revolt of the Rhine, when the garrison of Novaesium was reduced to the *Legio VI Victrix* alone, considerable changes were made (cf. Fig. 47); their tendency was to provide the camp with more elaborate buildings, both for headquarters and for the associations whose growth was fostered by the new regime. The *praetorium* and *quaestorium* were thrown into one, and a palatial residence was built for the commanding officer, with a garden and peristyle; to the west of the *praetorium* the treasury of the legion and the sanctuary of the *signa*, which we must suppose to have been in the *praetorium* itself before *A.D.* 70, were housed in a spacious building which took the place of the *strigae*. At the eastern end of the *principia* we find a colonnaded hall, which can hardly be anything but a *schola*.

★★★★★★

The auxiliary force having been reduced, there were fewer officers quartered in the camp. Nevertheless, a fresh dwelling-house was erected behind the *principia* on the site of some cavalry barracks. This may have been for the *praefectus castrorum*.

★★★★★★

In the Flavian period its chief use may have been for the purposes of military instruction, for we are still far from the days when each grade of the service was permitted to build a club-room under this name, as in the later camp at Lambaesis. Even at Novaesium it is possible that some of the other buildings of uncertain use belonging to the later period were *scholae*. The region adjoining the *porta praetoria* was occupied by *horrea* or magazines. It would seem that those to the west of the gate were hurriedly built during the revolt of Civilis, and burnt by the rebels; to the east of the gate is a large magazine with double flooring which is shown by tile-stamps to have been the handiwork of the Sixth Legion. It should not be forgotten that to each legion was assigned a *territorium* of greater or less extent, which furnished fodder, pasture, and firewood; amongst the civil duties of the legion was the management of this property—the *prata legionis* of which we read in inscriptions.

Finally, the luxury of the declining days of Rome's military power has left its trace in the suite of *thermae* erected on the ruins of the deserted camp of the legions by the *exercitus Germaniae inferioris*, as the tile-stamps call it. This no doubt was the force which built the third-century fort.

In order to complete the picture of a permanent camp under the Empire, we must borrow some features from that of Lambaesis in Numidia, built under Hadrian as the headquarters of the *Legio III Augusta*, which formed the garrison of North Africa throughout the Imperial period. The remains of a second and smaller camp about 2 km. to the west, which was temporarily occupied by the legion, are chiefly interesting by reason of the fact that on a monument in the centre of the encampment was inscribed the text of the speech delivered by Hadrian when he inspected the *Legio III Augusta* and other troops on July 1, *A. D.* 128. The smaller camp was doubtless used as a parade-ground on such occasions.

The *praetentura* of the larger camp, which has been completely excavated, presents a picture with which we are already familiar. Bordering on the *via principalis* we have a row of houses for the use, probably, of the *legatus legionis* (for whom no quarters seem to have been available in the *praetorium*) and the staff officers. Behind this *scamnum*, and separated from it by a narrow street parallel with the *via principalis*, are the quarters of the legionary *cohorts*, disposed on much the same plan as those of Novaesium, with a double *portico* in the centre and *contubernia* consisting of an inner and outer chamber (the latter quite small)

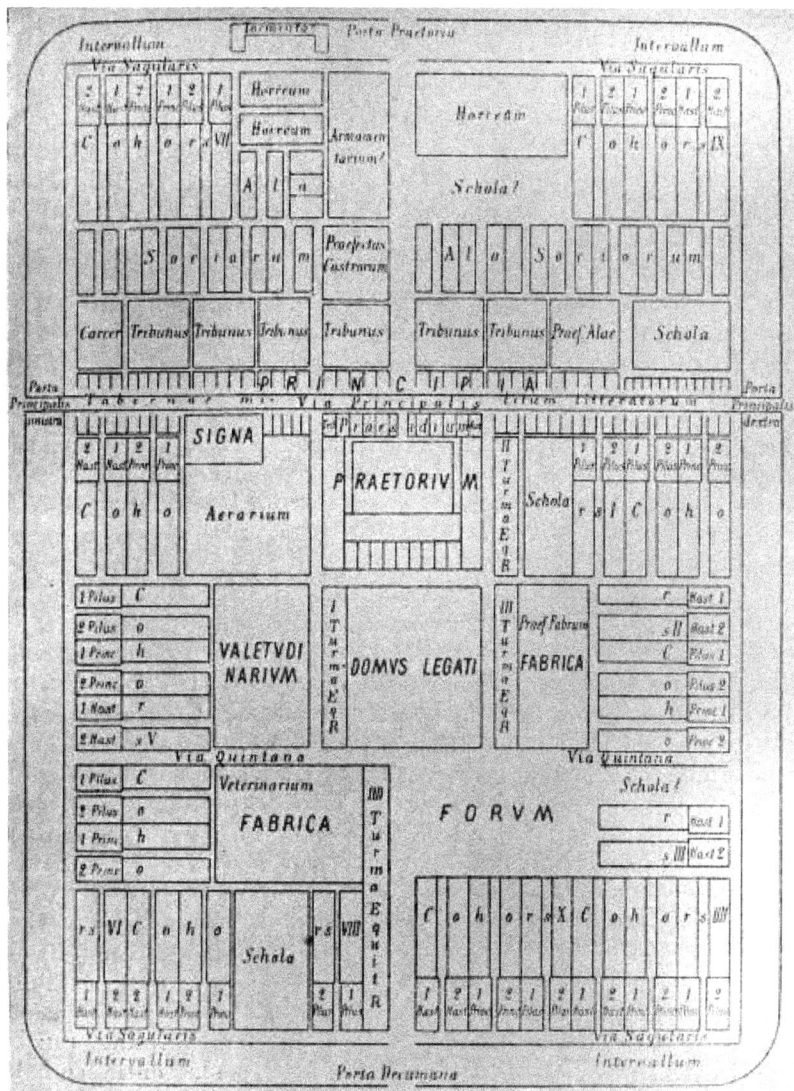

FIG. 47. The camp at Novaesium after A. D. 70 (from Nissen).

on either side. Inscriptions have been found with dedications 'to the *genius* of the century', which belonged to these barracks; one of them is dated in the joint reign of Septimius Severus and Caracalla, and this is at least as early as any of those which have come to light.

The fact is important, because it has been held that when Severus (as Herodian tells us) permitted the soldiers 'to live with their wives',

137

the camp became a mere parade-ground and headquarters building, and the quarters of the troops were replaced by clubrooms, &c. We now see that this was not so—or at least that a substantial number of troops continued to live in the camp itself. Beside the barrack buildings, the *praetentura* also contained stables and *horrea* which have no peculiar features.

The plan of the *praetorium*, or headquarters building, can be traced with certainty; and the walls of its imposing entrance hall, shown on Pl. XLI, are still standing. (This building is popularly called the *praetorium*; its true destination was not discovered in the earlier excavations). This hall is built over the *via principalis* at its intersection with the *via praetoria*, from which it is entered by a fine archway of three bays flanked by columns, bearing an inscription in honour of Septimius Severus; in fact, the scheme of the building is borrowed from that of the triumphal arch with four entrances, such as that of Theveste (Pl. XX a).

It served as the entrance to a large rectangular paved court, measuring 65 by 37.40 metres, and bordered on three sides by a *portico* of Doric columns upon which opened a series of small rooms. (1 These formed the armoury and arsenal of the legions. Inscriptions with the words *arma antesignana* and *postsignana* have been found in some, and sling-bullets and stone projectiles in others. At each corner of the court stood a drinking-fountain; and it doubtless also contained honorary monuments; the remains of an *Ara disciplinae* which now stand in it may, however, have been brought from elsewhere. The side facing the entrance hall is bounded by a wall, 1.75 m. high, supporting a platform approached by two nights of steps; and at the back of this is a second and shallower court, about which are grouped a number of halls and other buildings.

A Corinthian *portico* traverses the court, and in front of each of its columns is a pedestal upon which an Imperial statue once stood; the earliest was set up to Hadrian in *A.D.* 129. In the centre of the side which faces the entrance is an apsidal hall, beneath which are cellars; this was the *sacellum*, in which the *signa* of the legion were kept and worshipped, and the cellars contained the treasure, including the savings of the soldiers, which, as we are told by ancient authors, were deposited under the protection of the *signa*. We shall find in the frontier forts of the Empire precisely the same arrangement. The rooms to the right and left of this sanctuary are shown by the inscriptions found therein to have been the *scholae* or club-rooms (there may have

Entrance court of the *praetorium* at Lambaesis.

been an upper storey, but this is not quite certain), of various corps or grades: thus, on the left the *equites legionis* had their *schola*, and beyond them the non-commissioned officers, or *principales*, attached to the legionary *tribunes*; while various groups of *principales* attached to the staff had their club-rooms on the right of the central *sacellum*. The *tabularium*, or office, of the legion can also be located in one of the side-rooms; and a number of fragmentary inscriptions show that practically every grade of *principales* was permitted to have its *schola* from the time of Septimius Severus, whose constant aim was to increase the attractiveness of the service.

It must be observed that although no permanent legionary camps of the Republican period survive, the recent excavations at Numantia show that during the famous siege of that town by Scipio Aemilianus (134-133 B.C.) the principal points in the lines of circumvallation were occupied by *castella* built on the model of the *castra hiberna*. In one of these (which measures 130 x 140 metres) the *strigae* and *scamna* are in part well-preserved, and conform to the scheme above described. We have, for example, *strigae* 22½ metres broad, divided into three strips of equal breadth—the central lane and two rows each of six *contubernia*, which had an outer and inner room, each three metres square. Allowing ten men to each *contubernium*, the *striga* would give room for a *manipulus* of 2 x 60 = 120 men; and the camp was probably designed for one *cohort* and one *turma* of horse.

§ 6. Frontier Defences.

The conception of a scientific frontier was foreign to the government of the Roman Republic. From the force of circumstances rather than from settled policy the territory ruled by Rome and the sphere of her direct or indirect influence was constantly extended. In the closing half-century of senatorial rule vast regions were added to the Empire by the conquests of ambitious generals; but of these Pompey at least, by his refusal to treat the Euphrates as the limit of Roman dominion, at once showed that he had no definite idea of a frontier in the East and bequeathed to his successors a problem of enormous difficulty. Caesar, if the story told by Plutarch be true, proposed to return from his projected Parthian expedition by the shores of the Caspian, the Black Sea, and the Baltic, and to 'make the circle of Empire conterminous with ocean'; but this fantastic tale is scarcely worthy of credence.

With the advent of Augustus to power all was changed. For the first time it was recognised that a consistent frontier policy must be framed and followed; and the principle which Augustus bequeathed to his successor—*coercendum intra terminos imperium*—sounded the death-knell of indefinite expansion. Tacitus tells us (*Ann.* i. 9) that amongst his achievements men counted that of confining the Empire within the limits of 'sea, ocean, and distant rivers': if we add to this deserts, we shall not be far from the truth, for in his final conception the Rhine and Danube were regarded as forming the northern frontier, though the line of the Danube cannot be said to have been held in a military sense, and on the other hand the right bank of the Rhine remained throughout a great part of its length in Roman occupation even when the project of extending Roman rule to the Elbe was definitely abandoned. It is in this district that we meet with the earliest use of the term *limes*, which was in time to become synonymous with frontier, by a gradual change of meaning which connotes a change of policy.

In its original significance *limes* denotes a military road, such as the Romans constructed when opening up a newly conquered territory. Such were the roads made under Augustus, which ascended the valleys of the Lippe and the Main, and were doubtless intended to pave the way for the conquest of Western Germany. These *limites* were protected by *castella* occupied by 'auxiliary' regiments, such as the *castellum Lupiae flumini adpositum* of Tacitus (*Ann.* ii. 7), which is probably to be identified with Aliso (mentioned by Tacitus in the same chapter). The remains of such *castella* have been found in the valley of the Lippe at Haltern and Oberaden (both of which sites have been identified with Aliso), and in that of the Main at Höchst. In such cases the word *limes*, which is derived from the vocabulary of the land-surveyor, has not the sense of 'boundary', but that of 'track'. *Aperire* (*Vell.* ii. 120) or *scindere limitem* (Tac. *Ann.* i. 50) simply means 'to clear a track' through a pathless forest, such as those of Northern Germany, in order to render the communications of an advancing force easier and more secure.

In writings of the Trajanic and later periods, we find the word *limes* used in the sense of 'frontier'. Tacitus, for example, speaking of Domitian's defeat by the Dacians, says (*Agr.* 41), *Nec iam de limite imperii et ripa sed de hibernis legionum et possessione dubitatum.* Here the words *et ripa* seem to be explanatory of those which precede, so that no special system of frontier defence is implied. There can be no doubt, however, that it was the adoption of such a system which brought about the change in the meaning of the word *limes*. Under the Julio-Claudian dynasty there was no attempt to extend Roman rule beyond the Rhine; on the contrary, shortly after the withdrawal of three of the Rhine legions for the conquest of Britain, Claudius ordered all garrisons to be withdrawn from the right bank (Tac. *Ann.* xi. 19).

A strip of land was, however, reserved for the use of the legions, (*Ann.*) and no encroachment upon this was permitted to the German tribes. Tiles were manufactured in the brickfields of the right bank (*tegularia Transrhenana*), and in the regions occupied by friendly tribes, such as the Wetterau and Taunus, where the Mattiaci remained faithful to Rome until the revolt of Civilis. (The Castellum Mattiacorum built by Drusus preserves its name as Kastel, the *tête-de-pont* opposite Mainz, which was the headquarters of the Upper German Army; Tacitus, *Ann.* i.) Roman troops were employed in exploiting the natural resources of the country (*Ann.*). In the reign of Vespasian began the forward movement whose object was to cut off the re-entrant angle of the Rhine-Danube frontier. In *A. D.* 73-4 the thinly-populated district between the Rhine and the Neckar was occupied.

In recording this movement—the details of which are entirely unknown to us—Tacitus (*Germ.* 29) uses the phrase *limite acto promotisque praesidiis*. The *limites* here mentioned were the military roads which started from the legionary camps at Strassburg (Argentoratum) and Windisch (Vindonissa) and met at Rottweil, where a centre of the Imperial worship for the newly annexed territory was set up under the name of the 'Flavian altars' (*Arae Flaviae*). The military roads were prolonged as far as Tuttlingen on the Danube and Rottenburg on the Neckar (see Map 7), and the *praesidia* mentioned by Tacitus are to be seen in the earth forts of Waldmössingen, Rottweil, Sulz, and Rottenburg (see Map 7).

Still, however, the *limites* retained the function of tracks by which the newly conquered district was penetrated rather than that of boundaries. Ten years later, however, Domitian took in hand the question of the Main valley and the Taunus. In *A. D.* 83 he led an expedition in person against the Chatti, and drove them from their seats in the Taunus range. He then established a chain of frontier defences which Frontinus, writing a few years later, describes in the words *limitibus per cxx milia passuum actis, subiecit ditioni suae Jiostes quorum refugia nudaverat*. This was the beginning of the system of frontier defence which in time was carried from the Rhine to the Danube, and has in modern times been called 'the *limes' par excellence*.

From a point on the Rhine opposite Brohl a frontier track ran south-eastwards, crossing the Lahn, till it reached the western extremity of the Taunus, from which point it ran along the summit of the range, then turning southward, struck the Main at Kesselstadt (see Map 7). Along this line were built small earth forts, on the average about 85 metres square: the remains of these have been found beneath those of the stone forts which at a later date took their place (for example, at the Saalburg—here the earth fort measures 33 x78 m., while the stone fort which took its place measured 221 x 147 m.), and we know at least one instance (at Seckmauern) where the original earth fort was never built over. Between the forts were wooden watch-towers, and some traces of a fence have been discovered. But Domitian did not trust wholly in so weak a line of defence.

In rear of this *limes* were built a series of stone forts (at Hofheim, Heddernheim, Okarben, and Friedberg), large enough to accommodate a *cohors quingenaria*, from which the frontier forts could be quickly reinforced, and upon which the garrisons, if hard pressed, could fall back. They were connected by a system of roads, and the chief highway of the district, which followed the valley of the Main, was secured by stone forts at Höchst, Frankfurt, and Kesselstadt. (The length of this frontier-line, from Rheinbrohl to Kesselstadt, corresponds pretty accurately with the 120 Roman miles of Frontinus).

The strength of these defences was soon put to the test, for in *A. D.* 88-9 the *commandant* of the camp at Mainz, L. Antonius Saturninus, was proclaimed emperor by the Fourteenth and Twenty-First Legions, and the revolting troops were aided by the Chatti, who burst through the line of forts and made their way down the valleys of the Lahn and the Main: several of the earth forts on the *limes*, and one at least of the stone base forts (at Okarben), bear traces of having been partially destroyed by fire and rebuilt. The revolt was, however, speedily suppressed.

Domitian now determined to link up the northern *limes* with the district annexed by Vespasian. A glance at the map will show that for a considerable part of the distance the Main and Neckar formed a natural boundary; only where the line of defence crosses the Odenwald (between Wörth, on the Main, and Wimpffen, on the Neckar) was a *limes* and chain of forts similar to those of the Taunus necessary. This is precisely what we find; and there can be no doubt that this extension was due to Domitian. On the rivers, however, we find not earth but stone forts; but this is not of necessity to be interpreted as a mark of later elate. Where the frontier was strengthened by a river, it was thought safe to place the *cohort*-camps in the front line, while in

LIMES Germaniae et Raetiae.

Brohl
Niederbieber
Andernach
Neuwied
Koblenz
Niederberg

Butzbach
Arnsburg
Langenhain
Friedberg
Saalburg
Oberflorstadt
Feldberg
Marköbel
Heddernheim
Kesselstadt
Höchst
Hofheim
Zugmantel
Wiesbaden
Frankfurt
Gr. Krotzenburg

Bingen
Bingium
Mainz
Mogontiacum
Castel
Gr. Gerau
Stockstadt
Niedernberg
Obernburg

Worth
Lützelbach
Worms
Borbetomagus
Hesselbach
Milten
Mannheim
Ladenburg
Wald
Neuenheim
Obr. Scheid
Heidelberg
Neckarburken
Ost
Wimpfen
Böckingen
Wohlheim
Benningen
Karlsruhe
Cannstatt
Haqf
Pforzheim
Stuttgart
Zabern
Köngen
Tres Tabernae
Aureliae
Strassburg
Argentoratum
Rottenburg
Salz
Waldmössingen
Rottweil
Arae Flaviae
Freiburg
Tuttlingen

Ill
Rhein

Bâle
Constanz
Augst
Windisch
Augusta Rauracorum
Vindonissa
Zürich

Moselle

R. V. Darbishire, Oxford, 1907

MAP 7

Modulus 1 : 2,000,000.

Milia Passuum Rom.
0 10 20 30 40 50

Milaria Anglica
0 10 20 30 40 50

Kilometres
0 10 20 30 40 50

Limes ━━━━━   Viae ......

Würzburg

Nürnberg

Castra Regina
Regensburg

Damba   Theilenhofen
         Weissenburg
Weilbnger   Pfünz
              Eining
              Pföring

Mainhart
Murrhart
Buch
Aalen
Unter Böbingen

Uespring

Faimingen

Ulm

Augsburg
Augusta Vindelicorum

München

Isar

Abudiacum

Kempten
Cambodunum

Bregenz
Brigantium

Inn

Innsbruck

a district such as the Odenwald we may be sure that there were base forts in which bodies of troops were held in reserve. But even here we find *cohort*-camps at Ober-Scheidental and Neckarburken.

In any case, there can be little doubt that Vespasian's line was prolonged northwards by Köngen to Cannstadt and a continuous chain of defence established. It does not, however, follow that this marked the limit of Roman occupation. A Greek inscription found at Rottenburg (Sumelocenna) mentions differences with a procurator of the district (probably = *tractus*) of Sumelocenna and that beyond the *limes*, which formed part of the Imperial domains; and this suggests that the function of a *limes* was not altogether military; the regulation of traffic and intercourse between barbarian and Roman was also made easy thereby.

In our own island the reign of Domitian likewise saw the beginnings of a system of frontier defence. In *A. D.* 78 and the following years Gn. Julius Agricola, as Governor of Britain, reduced to submission a number of tribes hitherto independent of Rome. Tacitus tells us (*Agr.* 20. 3) that at the close of his second campaign he secured the conquered districts by a line of *praesidia* and *castella*; this may have occupied the site of the wall from Tyne to Solway to be discussed later. In *A. D.* 81 he reached the estuaries of Forth and Clyde, and here again a line of *praesidia* was established (*Agr.* 23), which have not perished without leaving traces of their existence. The clearest are to be found at Bar Hill, a station on the line of Antoninus Pius's rampart.

Below the level of the Antonine *castellum* were found the ditches surrounding an earth fort measuring 191 x 160 feet. The inner ditch, about 9 feet wide by 4½ feet deep, had but one entrance, on the eastern side. The outer ditch is somewhat irregular in outline; it is ingeniously doubled in front of the main entrance of the fort. We can subscribe to the eulogy of Tacitus, who tells us that experts remarked the sagacity shown by Agricola in choosing sites (*Agr.* 22); but as a system of defence for the newly-won territory a chain of posts so weakly held as these must have been, could have had little value. They could have received but little support from their distant base in case of serious attack, and probably depended upon the fleet for supplies.

★★★★★★

At Newstead, near Melrose, an important station commanding the passage of the Tweed, the remains of a large fort have been excavated. There are traces of at least four successive occupations, the earliest of which dates to the time of Agricola. It served as a base fort for the time from Clyde to Forth.

★★★★★★

The reign of Trajan is notable rather for the extension of the territories of Rome than for any measures of systematic defence; but it is to be observed that he lavished time and money on the construction of great military highways along the frontier lines, trusting, as it would seem, mainly in the rapid concentration of overwhelming forces to paralyse hostile inroads. The most famous of these was that which connected the Rhine frontier with the Danube, the defence of which presented an increasingly serious problem. A late biographer speaks of it as a 'road through fierce peoples easily traversed from the Black Sea to Gaul' (Aurelius Victor, *Caes*. 13); and Trajan himself, in the famous inscription carved on the rock of Orsova, where the road is carried through the Iron Gates on an artificial shelf cut in the sheer cliff, tells how he 'cleft mountains and cut off projecting crags'.

From Cannstadt, an important post on the *limes*, connected with Mainz by a route which dates from the reign of Domitian, two roads led to the Upper Danube. One of these ascended the valley of the Fils, crossed the watershed to Urspring, and was carried on to the Danube at Faimingen, which was connected with the important town of Augusta Vindelicorum (Augsburg). This, however, soon ceased to mark the limit of Roman occupation: the *limes* proper was formed by a road, dating from Trajan's time, which ran up the valley of the Rems to Aalen and followed the northern edge of the Jura, then descended into the valley of the Altmühl, which it crossed at Pfünz, reaching the Danube at Eining. From this point to the Black Sea the *limes* followed the course of the river.

It was not only on the north that Trajan pursued this policy. In North Africa the gradual extension of the pacified area is marked by the construction of military roads. The highway from Theveste to Lambaesis may be regarded as a link in the chain of defence which secured the corn-growing lands of the province of Africa: but it formed only the inner line, since as early as *A. D* 97 we find Roman troops in the region of the Shotts. (This is proved by an inscription found in 1891, between the Shott-el-Djerid and the Shott-el-Gharsa). And in *A. D.* 105 a road, which may be regarded as the *limes* of the provinces, was constructed to the south of the Aurés range, which on the west commanded the outlet at Bescera (Biskra) and on the east was linked with the highway which since Augustus's reign had connected Theveste, Capsa, and Tacape, and served as a frontier line. The coast road was about the same time prolonged to Leptis.

In the East the incorporation of the territory of the Nabataean Arabs in the Empire (a. d. 105) created a fresh frontier-problem; and here too Trajan's first step was to construct a military highway with strong posts at intervals; the remains of these—at Odruh, El-leggun and El-Kastal—show that auxiliary *cohorts* supplied the frontier garrisons. At a somewhat later date an outer chain of forts (scarcely 20 miles to the east) was added. What steps were taken to protect the newly won province of Dacia we are not able to say: on the east the line of the Aluta was certainly held.

With the reign of Hadrian, we come to a turning-point in the history of the frontiers. Not only is the period of expansion abruptly closed, but a systematic attempt is made to fence the Empire about with permanent barriers, where such were not furnished by the hand of nature. Hadrian's biographer tells us that 'where the barbarians were separated from the Empire not by rivers but by *limites*, he kept them out by means of tall stakes planted deep and joined together after the fashion of a wall-like hedge'. (*Vita Hadr.*) Such a palisade, consisting in split oak-trunks standing 9 feet high, implanted in a ditch 4½ feet deep, and bound together on the inside by cross-beams, has left its traces throughout the whole length of the *limes* from Rhine to Danube, and may be certainly identified as the work of Hadrian.

Its military value may be called in question, but for the control of traffic and intercourse between Roman and barbarian it was doubtless effective. It would seem, however, that Hadrian held it of sufficient defensive importance to justify the abandonment of the elaborate system of base forts devised by Domitian. The auxiliary regiments were now quartered in large stone forts erected (as *e. g.* at the Saalburg) on the site of the old earth forts on the *limes* itself, (at the same time stone watch-towers took the place of wooden ones); and base forts such as Friedberg and Heddernheim were dismantled. At the same time the windings of the old frontier were, as far as possible, replaced by straight lines, in order to give direct communication between the frontier forts.

The work of Hadrian on the Raeto-Germanic *limes* does not stand by itself. In other parts of the Empire we find the same system of mechanical barriers, which in their earliest form may generally be attributed to Hadrian. That the line of fortifications which crosses Northern Britain from Tyne to Solway was traced by him is an undoubted fact: but it is by no means so easy to determine what was the original nature of the barrier here set up. It is well known that the existing remains are those of a stone wall with forts (to be described later), to the south of which is an earthwork, or *vallum*, as shown in Fig. 48. The *vallum* consisted in a fosse 7 or 8 feet deep, 30 feet wide at the top and about 15 at the bottom, with two high ramparts to north and south and a third and much lower one, possibly due to a later clearing of the fosse, on the southern edge.

Behind the forts it has been worn down and sometimes filled up. Between the *vallum* and the stone wall ran a military road. So far as external evidence goes, it points to the conclusion that Hadrian's fortification consisted, neither in stone wall nor *vallum*, but in a turf rampart; since the biographer of Antoninus Pius (5, 3) tells us that that emperor raised a *second* turf-wall in Britain.

******

Forts similar to those on the *limites* were also planted in the hilly districts of Britain, whose inhabitants were of doubtful loyalty. Thus, a number of auxiliary *castella* have been discovered in Wales, one of which—at Gelligaer—is a remarkably perfect example of the type; and there were others in the mountainous country of the Brigantes (mod. Yorkshire and Derbyshire), such as those of Brough and 'Melandra Castle', near Glossop.

******

And remains of such a *murus caespiticius* have in fact been discovered in the neighbourhood of the station of Amboglanna (Birdoswald), which it seems reasonable to identify with the work of Hadrian. The problem of the *vallum* is a more difficult one, and has not yet received a satisfactory solution. It is hard to see that it could ever have possessed much value as a military defence, and it seems more probable that it marked a line of civil frontier.

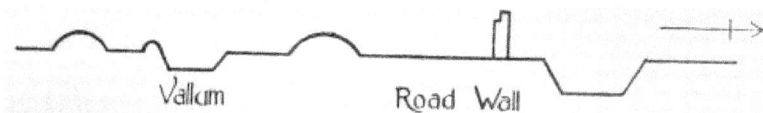

Fig. 48. Section of wall and *vallum* in Northern Britain.

In the Danube provinces, too, the work of Hadrian may be traced with much probability. From Kustendje (Costanza, the ancient Tomi) on the Black Sea to a point south of Crnavoda on the Danube, a series of defensive works span the Dobrudja. We find a larger and a smaller earthwork: the former of these is the more northerly, and is protected

149

by earth forts at intervals of about 1 kilometre, while the southern *vallum* has no adjuncts save a ditch on the south side. There is also a *stone* wall, the line of which crosses and recrosses the northern *vallum*, and is clearly later in date. The northern *vallum*, which, like the German palisade, takes as direct a course as possible, may be assigned to Hadrian; as for the southern earthwork, it may perhaps be due to barbarian rather than Roman hands. The province of Dacia also had its *limes*. Where the River Aluta formed the boundary, no special defences needed to be constructed: and the same may be said of the northern boundary of the province where that was formed by the Szamos; but abundant traces exist of an artificial barrier running from Tiho to Kis-Sebes. The method of construction varies: sometimes we find a stone Avail, at others a palisade, or again a fosse and dyke, or even a mere *vallum* without a ditch. The difficult questions arising from this diversity of construction have not yet been settled; but the inception of the undertaking can hardly belong to any other time save that of Hadrian.

It is to be noted that the *limites* thus traced were not coincident with the extreme limit of military occupation. Outside the *vallum* of the Dobrudja was the legionary camp of Troesmis: to the east of the Aluta irregular corps such as the Syrian archers and the *burgarii et veredarii Daciae inferioris* had fortified stations; to the north of the British *limes* such positions as Bremenium (High Rochester) were strongly held. All these facts lend colour to the view that the function of the mechanical barrier was as much civil as military.

It is very probable that the works described above belong to the earliest years of Hadrian's reign. Almost his first act was to regulate the affairs of the Lower Danube; and he appears to have visited Germany in *A.D.* 121, and Britain, where the destruction of the Ninth Legion called for his presence, in *A.D.* 122. It is not so clear whether the advance of the German *limes* belongs to the latter years of his reign or to that of his successor, who certainly built a chain of forts to the east of the Aluta as advanced posts for the defence of Lower Dacia, and likewise extended the area of military occupation in Britain by the construction of an earthen rampart from the Forth to the Clyde, with forts at intervals ranging from (roughly) 2,500 to 4,800 yards. It doubtless followed fairly closely the line of Agricola's *praesidia*—although one of these, at Camelon, lies a little to the north of it—in fact, as has already been mentioned, we find the stone fort of the second century built on the site of the earlier earthwork at Bar Hill.

The *Vallum* was constructed, as is shown by the inscriptions found on its course, by detachments of the Second, Sixth, and Twentieth Legions—the first *cohort* of Tungrians is also mentioned—acting under the orders of Q. Lollius Urbicus, Governor of Britain about *A.D.* 140-2. It stretched from Chapel Hill, near Old Kilpatrick, on the Clyde, to Bridgeness, near Carriden, on the Forth, a distance of about 36½ miles. Towards the extremities all traces of it have ceased to exist: but for a considerable part of its course the outline of the fosse is traceable, and in some places the whole structure is well preserved. The defences consisted in:

(*a*) The outer mound, formed by the upcast from the fosse. This is irregular in shape, usually flat-topped where the ground is level, but higher and with a narrower crown when the ground slopes northwards.

(*b*) The fosse, which is V-shaped (*fastigata*), but has the peculiarity that both scarp and counter-scarp, which are inclined at an angle of from 26° to 30°, have a perpendicular drop of a foot or so from the lowest point, so that the bottom of the ditch is flat. The average depth was about 12 feet, the width varies from 20 feet (where the *vallum* runs along the foot of a hill) to 40 feet, which is normal. The counterscarp is artificially heightened.

(*c*) The berm, a flat ledge about 25 feet wide between the rampart and the ditch. The width is in excess of that usually formed in Roman fortifications, and has not been satisfactorily explained.

(*d*) The rampart or *vallum* proper. This was 14 feet in thickness, resting on a stone base—rubble enclosed by two lines of squared freestone kerbs. (It was drained at intervals by culverts). It was built of sods, laid probably grass to grass, as is shown by the dark horizontal lines which are seen in sections, representing the decayed vegetable matter on the surface of the sods. The original height of the *vallum* is a matter of conjecture, but as its sides must have been battered for safety, and the top can scarcely have been less than 6 feet in width, we may perhaps assume that it was from 10 to 12 feet high.

About 40 or 50 yards to the south of the rampart ran a military highway, about 17 feet broad, which served as a means of communication between the forts.

In the latter half of the second century *A. D.* the tide of barbarism began to turn against Rome. It was all that Marcus could do to maintain the Danube frontier against the Marcomanni, Quadi, and Iazyges; we are told that he contemplated the annexation of the territory occupied by these tribes, and the formation of new provinces under the names of Marcomannia and Sarmatia, and a glance at the map of Central Europe will show that the occupation of the Northern Carpathians and the Bohemian quadrilateral, *if an adequate force could be spared for their defence,* would have given the Empire an impregnable barrier against its northern foes.

But the task was too great for the rulers of the time; and with the advent of the new dynasty of the Severi we come to the last phase in the construction of mechanical barriers. In Britain the outer line of defence fortified by Antoninus Pius was abandoned—the finds indicate that the stations were never occupied after the reign of Commodus—and the Hadrianic *limes* received its final shape as a solid wall of rubble faced with *opus quadratum,* averaging about 8 feet in thickness, and probably in origin about 17 feet high. It is this wall whose remains form so conspicuous a monument of Roman rule in Britain, often but, as it would seem, wrongly, ascribed to Hadrian.

At intervals of 1,000 Roman paces, as nearly as the nature of the ground permits, as well as at the points needing special protection, such as river-crossings or defiles, we find small forts—commonly termed mile-castles—measuring about 60 by 50 feet, built in massive masonry, with gates in their northern and southern sides; and between the mile-castles were turrets for sentries, three to a mile, recessed in the wall itself. But the chief protection was afforded by the seventeen *cohort*-camps, the list of which, with that of the troops which formed their garrisons, is furnished by the *Notitia Dignitatum.* It is impossible here to do more than describe a characteristic example of these forts, which may serve to typify the frontier-stations of the Roman Empire.

We may take for our example the *cohort*-camp of Borcovicus or Borcovicus (Housesteads), where the systematic excavations of Prof. Bosanquet in 1898 have made it possible to trace the disposition of its parts with accuracy (cf. Fig. 49). We know, moreover, that Borcovicus was garrisoned from first to last by the *cohors prima Tungrorum,* which was a *cohors miliaria,* nominally 1,000 strong, but was not, like the second regiment of Tungrians, which was also quartered in Northern Britain, furnished with a cavalry contingent.

★★★★★★

The Tungrian *cohorts,* as their name shows, were originally raised on the Rhine. They took part in the civil war of *A. D.* 69 (Tac. *Hist.* ii. 14 f.), and are found in Britain as early as the time of Agricola, under whom they served with distinction, notably in the Battle of the Mons Graupius in *A. D.* 83 (Tac. *Agr.* 36).

★★★★★★

The fort stands on the very edge of the basaltic cliff, forming the escarpment of the wall, which coincides with its northern front. It is oblong in shape, measuring 610 feet by 367, and in this respect departs from the usual type which is square or nearly so. Possibly it may have been lengthened by extension to the west, as there is reason to think that other forts on the wall—Cilurnum (Chesters) and Amboglanna (Birdoswald)—were increased in length by additions projecting to the north of the wall.

The walls of the fort, which were strengthened internally by an embankment of earth to the height of five feet and an inner reclaiming-wall enclose a space of nearly five acres. (This inner reclaiming-wall is broken at certain points by buildings, *e.g.* the latrines, which were immediately to the west of the south-east angle-tower, see Plan). The corners were, as usual, rounded, with angle towers. Two towers have also been discovered on the east and one on the south side, and others flanked the four gates by which the fort was entered. All the gates had originally double entrances, but towards the close of the Roman occupation each had one of its passages blocked. If we adopt the nomenclature of the legionary camp, we must call the north and south gates the *portae principales*, in spite of the fact that the former is that which faces hostile territory, and the street which connects them the *via principalis*. In the centre of this street we find on the western side the *principia* or headquarters building (x) (Often, but less correctly, styled *praetorium*). During the later Roman occupation this underwent considerable alterations, but excavation has made it possible to trace the original plan.

The *principia* measured 89½ feet by 76 feet 4 in., and were partly built on an artificial platform, owing to the slope of the site. An arched entrance led into an outer court (4), which on three sides was bordered by a *portico* 9½ feet deep supported by stone columns and angle-piers, and covered with a slate roof sloping inwards.

Opposite to the entrance was a doorway 12 feet wide, spanned by an arch leading into an inner court (7), 30 feet deep, bordered on the outer side only by a *portico* similar to that of the outer court with a central archway (6). The court had a lateral entrance on the northern

153

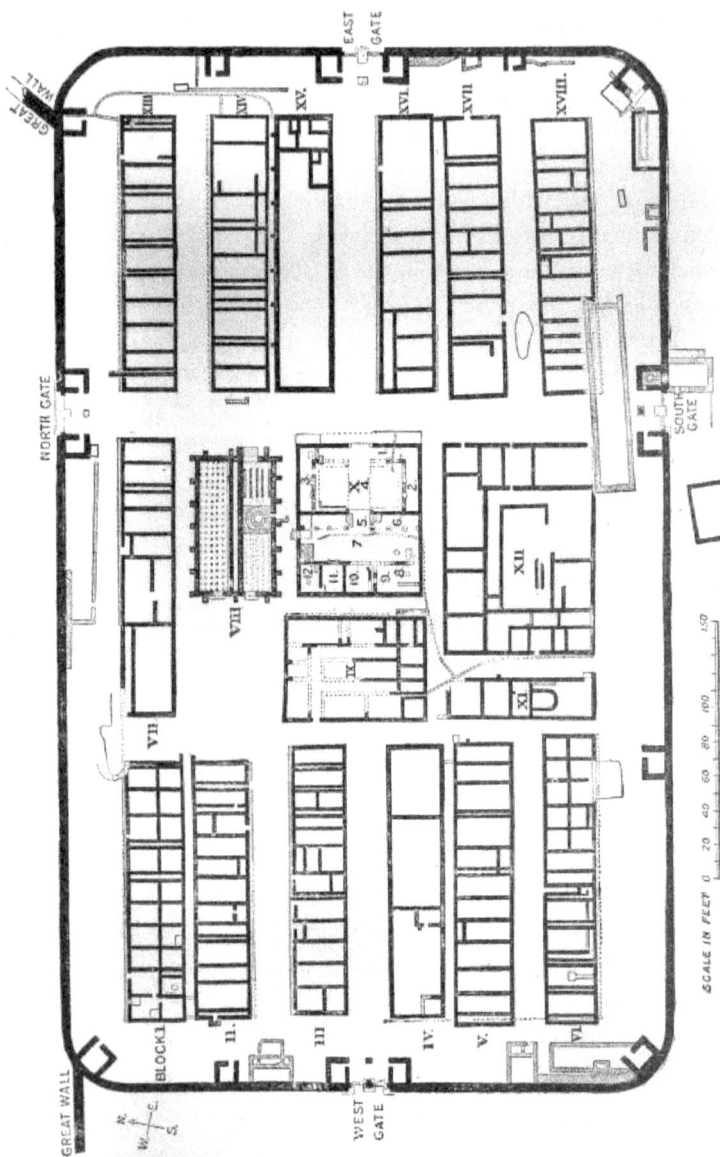

Fig. 49. Plan of fort at Housesteads (Borcovicus).

side, and possibly also on the south, though no trace of this remains. Facing this court was a row of five chambers (8-12), four of which had broad doorways opening on the court, whilst the corner chamber on the right (12) was entered by a side door in No. 11. The five chambers are a feature common to the *principia* of many Roman forts, and no doubt had well-defined functions. There can be no doubt that the central chamber was the *sacellum*, in which the *signa* were kept, and worshipped together with the genius of the regiment and the divinities of the Imperial House; amongst the other chambers we must seek the treasury of the *cohort* and the *tabularium*, where the accounts were kept.

It is a reasonable conjecture that where we find an artificially heated chamber we may recognise this latter room, where a staff of clerks (*librarii*) was constantly at work. At Borcovicus the plan of the five chambers was altered during the later occupation. Rooms 8 and 9 were thrown into one; the entrance of 8 was then blocked up and that of 9 contracted. The entrances of 11 was also blocked, so that 11 and 12 could only be approached through 10. There are signs that an upper floor was constructed in these chambers (this is a very unusual feature, it is conjecturally restored in the Saalburg, but on very doubtful evidence), and as a quantity of flue-tiles were found in the debris we may be sure that the *tabularium* is to be sought here. The lower floor of the innermost chamber will then be the strong-room, containing the archives and military chest. (In many forts an underground chamber beneath the *sacellum* formed the strong room). A large find of arrowheads was made in this angle; but this proves nothing as to the original destination of the chamber.

We now come to the quarters of the troops, which preserve the form of the *hemistrigium*, but when grouped in pairs were not back to back but face to face. A glance at the Plan will show the significance of this grouping. It will be seen that in each angle of the fort there were three *hemistrigia* (I-III, IV-VI, XIII-XV, XVI-XVIII), besides one in the centre of the north front (VII). Since two of these blocks, as we shall see, differ from the usual type (IV AND XV), and a third may have been destined for special purposes, there remain ten in which the ten companies (*centuriae*) of the *cohort* must have been housed. These were so disposed that the doors of the *contubernia* faced the rampart; and it is easy to see that in an advanced post exposed to sudden attack this arrangement was admirably suited for immediate defence, whereas in a permanent camp such as that of Novaesium (Chapter 3,

§ 5) the confinement of each *centuria* in a narrow *cul-de-sac* was more conducive to the maintenance of discipline.

It was not possible at Borcovicus to undertake a complete excavation of the blocks; but it was clear that, like those of Novaesium, they were divided into *contubernia*, ten or eleven in number. In one case the presence of a hearth seems to indicate the *centurion's* quarters at the end of the *hemistrigium*. The blocks vary in length, measuring 152-169 by 33-37 feet, so that the space allotted to each soldier but little exceeds that allowed by Hyginus for his imaginary field-force.

It has already been mentioned that two of the blocks presented special features. No. IV contained several pieces of iron slag and masses of burnt clay, showing that smelting works had been carried on therein. It was doubtless the *fabrica*. No. XV, a buttressed building, in which no partitions could be traced, had a small suite of baths at its eastern extremity. It may have been a *schola* in the later sense of the word. It remains to describe the buildings (other than the *praetorium*) in the centre of the fort. Immediately to the south of the *praetorium* was the residence of the *commandant* (XII), a building measuring 124 x 82½ feet. It has a central court with a corridor running round it, upon which the rooms opened. To the north of the *praetorium* were the storehouses or *horrea* (VIII). These consisted in two long and narrow buildings parallel with each other. They had thick walls strengthened with buttresses and floors raised in the one case on stone pillars, in the other on dwarf walls, which made them practically damp-proof. Such storehouses are a standing feature in the forts of Northern Britain, and are always placed in the latera praetor ii.

Behind the *horrea* was an open space, which we may conjecture to have been the *Forum* of the camp; whilst in the rear of the *praetorium* was a building somewhat resembling in its general plan the camp-hospital (*valetudinarium*) at Novaesium. Possibly it may have fulfilled the same function. A small building, 89 x 24 feet, containing an apsidal structure, stood behind the *commandant's* house, and in the centre of the north front was a *hemistrigium* which appears to have contained offices—perhaps the camp-prison may have been here.

The fort which we have described is typical of those which, in the second century *A.D.*, were erected on all the frontiers of the Empire. The first-century earth forts of the Flavian period have naturally left much less enduring traces. Their most interesting feature was the system of ditches—often threefold—with carefully protected entrances. Sometimes we find a straight ditch covering the gateway (described by Hyginus as a *titulus* or 'label'); or again, the rampart curves inwards as it approaches the entrance from the left side, so that an attacking party would be forced to expose their right sides as they neared the gateway. This is called by Hyginus the *clavicula* or 'bolt', and is found at Newstead.

Even in their remote garrison posts the Roman soldiers did not forego the amenities of civilized life. There was probably not a fort without its suite of baths. These *balnea* are occasionally found inside the *castellum*, but much more commonly in an 'annexe', itself as a rule defended by rampart and ditch. In these 'annexes'—of which there are as many as three attached to the fort at Newstead—dwelt the civil population which followed in the wake of the troops, forming a settlement similar (though smaller) to the *canabae* adjoining the legionary camps; and the baths were a kind of club frequented by the soldiers and their friends. Even the earth fort of Inchtuthil, which was probably occupied by the army of Agricola in its northerly advance, had an elaborate *balneum* more solid in its construction than the camp to which it belonged.

The wall in Northern Britain, if the most massive, was not the longest built by Roman engineers. In the eastern section of the Rhine-Danube *limes*—the *limes Raeticus*—we find a massive wall 175 km. in length, which must have been at least 2½ metres in height and is more than 1 metre wide; to make room for this Hadrian's palisade was destroyed. We cannot tell why the same plan was not adopted in the German section, where we find an earthen dyke and fosse, which did not take the place of the palisade, but were erected behind it.

In the Dobrudja the stone wall above mentioned, which is about 61 km. in length, is embedded in an earthen rampart with a ditch ten metres wide and three deep. The date of its construction is a matter of dispute, and many authorities hold it to be a work of the fourth century *A. D.*; we find fragments of architectural ornament from Tomi used in its construction, and this fact is certainly in favour of a late date. But the analogies of Britain and Germany would lead us rather to assign it to the time of the Severi.

The system of mechanical barriers was tried and found wanting in the wars of the third century *A. D.* Under Severus Alexander the German invaders broke through the *limes*, and actually crossed the Rhine; and although they were for a time driven back by Maximinus Thrax, the foothold of the Romans on the right bank of the river was henceforth precarious, and the Transrhenane possessions of Rome were irrecoverably lost under Gallienus. The 'Empire of the Gauls' was called into being by the stress of barbarian pressure: but all that it could do was to maintain the Rhine frontier.

In other parts of the Empire the term *limes* had now acquired a fresh signification—that of an open frontier protected by a chain of small blockhouses (*burgi*). The word is of Teutonic origin, and its derivative *burgarius* is found in an inscription dating from the close of Hadrian which mentions a *numerus burgariorum et veredariorum Pannoniae Inferioris* stationed in Lower Dacia. But the blockhouse system seems to owe its inception to Commodus, who, as an inscription records, fortified the right bank of the Danube in this way *ad clandestinos latrunculorum transitus*; while there is evidence to show that the same system was adopted in Africa. This became the normal mode of defence on the southern and eastern frontiers.

The *limites* were organised as independent military commands, and in the perfected scheme of Diocletian each was placed under a *dux*, while the garrison troops of the Empire bore the title of *limitanei*. Diocletian did much to provide the frontiers with fortified posts. On the upper Rhine, in Arabia and in Africa, we find the type of *castellum* which is characteristic of this period—square in outline with small posterns as well as the principal gateways. But a chain of *castella* and *burgi* is of little value against serious attack unless the defenders can be readily reinforced from a base in the rear: and this fact was not sufficiently recognised. Legionary camps were built on the *limites, e.g.* at El-leggum on the *limes Arabiae*, where the *Legio IV Martia Victrix* was quartered: and it must be supposed that the field-army (*comitatenses*) was regarded as an adequate support for the frontier garrisons. The history of the two centuries following Diocletian's reorganisation was to prove that this confidence was baseless.

§ 7. NAVAL WARFARE.

The early history of the Roman fleet is contained in a few scattered notices preserved chiefly by Livy. It is true that the story of a naval action fought on the Tiber in 426 B. C. is absurd, and rests on a misunderstanding of the term *classis*; but a 'long ship' (see below) is mentioned as conveying envoys to Delphi in 394 B. C, and whatever date we assign to the earliest treaty between Rome and Carthage, it can hardly be disputed that such instruments were negotiated in 348 and 306 B. C, and imply that Rome was already a naval power to be reckoned with in the western Mediterranean. In 338 B. C. the ships of the Antiates were taken and their beaks used to adorn the *rostra* (platform) of the *comitum* (public meeting place); and the ship's prow appears as a symbol on the Roman *aes grave* (bronze cast coins) from the earliest times.

It was not, however, until 311 B. C. that a special naval command was created. In that year *duoviri navales* (naval officers responsible for equipping the fleet) were appointed by decree of the people (though in the following year we find the Senate directing the commander of the fleet to operate on the Campanian coast), and we hear of them from time to time up till the second century B. C., when they disappear from history. They were only appointed when the need for their services arose. (It would seem that when *duoviri* were appointed, each was usually given a squadron often ships). The extension of Roman influence in South Italy, the war with Pyrrhus, and especially the operations against Tarentum (the Tarentines defeated the Roman fleet in 283 B. C., in which the Tarentines received the support of a Carthaginian fleet) brought home to the minds of the Romans the necessity for naval organisation, and in 267 B. C. four *quaestores classici* (low ranking magistrates) were for the first time elected. In later times we find that their several headquarters were at Ostia, Cales, Ravenna, and (probably) Lilybaeum in Sicily; but other duties (especially in connexion with the corn-supply) took the place of those for which they had first been appointed. Three years after their institution Rome became involved in the first and most important of her naval wars.

The narrative of the first Punic War in Polybius has been subjected to much criticism, and it seems that we must be sceptical as to the figures which he gives—e. g. the numbers of ships engaged in the Battle of Ecnomus (330 Roman, 350 Carthaginian). The stages of the war and the composition of the fleets are, however, clear.

In 264 B. C, at the outset of the war, the Romans built a hundred *quinqueremes* and twenty *tiremes*, and naval contingents were also furnished by their allies in South Italy. This fleet, commanded by G. Duilius, the consul of 260 B. C., won a considerable victory at Mylae over the Carthaginian force of 130 ships, commemorated by the erection of the Columna Rostrata. We are told that the Romans owed their success to the 'ravens' (*corvi*), or boarding-bridges lowered by a rope and block at the mast-head, and furnished with a spike which became fixed in the enemy's deck. (Some critics have cast doubt upon this story, believing it to be an invention of Fabius Pictor, the Roman annalist. They suggest that the *corvus* was really a grapnel, such as were in common use in the second Punic War).

The Carthaginian fleet, thus weakened in numbers, was again defeated at Tyndaris in 257 B. C. Carthage then resolved to make a determined effort to regain the command of the sea; Rome replied with a shipbuilding programme calculated, no doubt, to give her a margin of superiority; and the victories of Ecnomus (256 B. C.) and Hermaea (255 B. C.) would have established Rome's naval supremacy, but for the loss of all her battleships and prizes (save eighty) in a great storm soon after the last-named battle. The Romans lost no time in repairing their loss by fresh building; but we are told by Polybius that a second storm (in 253 B. C.) cost them 150 ships and forced them to 'retire from the sea'. The truth of this narrative has been suspected; and the course of events makes it clear that Rome did not in fact surrender her command of the sea. In 250 B. C. she undertook the siege and blockade of Lilybaeum, and had 243 ships at sea in the following year, when P. Claudius Pulcher lost ninety-three ships in the disaster of Drepana and others at Lilybaeum, while a second fleet under L. Junius was wholly destroyed by a storm.

Carthage was now unchallenged mistress of the waterways; but she neglected her golden opportunity, and in 242 B. C., by a supreme effort, the Romans put to sea with 200 *quinqueremes* built, as Polybius tells us, on the model of the ship of Hannibal the Rhodian, a famous pirate. This fleet, commanded by G. Lutatius Catulus, destroyed that of Carthage at the Battle of the Aegates Insulae (Mar. 10, 241 B.C.), and brought the war to an end.

The Romans were now masters of the sea, and in order to retain a hold on their oversea possessions—Sicily, acquired by the terms of peace, and Sardinia and Corsica, surrendered by Carthage three years later—they were obliged to maintain a standing fleet, in part furnished by their allies in Italy. In 228 B. C. they crushed the Illyrian pirates with a force of 200 *quinqueremes*, and thus first displayed their power in Eastern waters. The naval operations of the Hannibalic War were not of primary importance in determining its issue. No serious effort was made by Carthage to challenge Rome's naval supremacy or to harass her coast-line, while the command of the sea enabled Rome to invade Africa in force and thus bring Carthage to her knees.

By the terms of peace (201 B. C.) the Carthaginian fleet was surrendered, but only to be destroyed; and the Romans, having vanquished the chief naval power of the Mediterranean, no longer felt themselves bound to maintain an overwhelming force at sea. The history of the Roman navy in the second century b. c. is one of continuous decline, interrupted by outbursts of activity; moreover, Rome came to rely more and more on the forces supplied by her allies. The result of this was that by the close of the century, piracy was almost unchecked in the eastern Mediterranean (where Rhodes, which had kept it under control in the days of her power, had been reduced to impotence by Rome), and when in 89 B. C. Mithradates took the sea with a fleet estimated by Appian at 400 sail, the Romans were at once swept off the Aegean. It was only the energy of Lucullus, who gathered together a fleet from the Greek allies of Rome, and the naval skill of the Rhodians, that restored the balance of power. But the senatorial government was slow to learn its lesson; the scourge of piracy grew past bearing, and the attempts to suppress it were wholly inadequate.

At length in 67 B. C. the Lex Gabinia was passed, entrusting the command in Eastern waters to Pompey, and a new chapter in Roman naval history was begun. His fleet numbered 500 ships; the Mediterranean was divided into districts, each of which was patrolled by a squadron under a *legatiis*; the strongholds of the pirates were taken and turned into naval bases, and in three months the sea was cleared of their craft. Pompey relied on the forces supplied by the Greek and Asiatic coast-towns and islands, and on the nautical skill of their captains, especially the Rhodians; and in the earlier civil wars naval strength was on the side of the East.

At the outset Pompey controlled a fleet as large as that with which he had crushed the pirates, while Caesar could only put 150 ships on the sea, and his conduct of the campaign in Illyria, with Brundisium as a base, against enormous odds, was a triumph of genius assisted by good fortune. It was not, however, sea-power that determined the issues in this stage of the struggle. Pharsalus was decisive of the first war, just as Philippi ended the second, in spite of the fact that Brutus and Cassius, controlling the resources of the East, were far superior to the triumvirs in naval power.

Under Octavian's rule in Italy, however, the balance was shifted. Sextus Pompeius succeeded to the control of the fleet gathered by the Liberators, (he received the title of *praefectus classis et orae maritimae* from the Senate in April, 43 B.C, after the relief of Mutina); and Octavian was forced to realise that he must be met on his own element. Agrippa formed and trained a fleet of 300 ships in the land-locked basin formed by the junction of the Avernian and Lucrine lakes, and at Naulochus (36 B. C.) won a decisive victory over Pompeius. Five years later this same fleet, homogeneous in build, manned by crews trained on a definite system, and commanded by a single brain, defeated the more imposing (in size, not in numbers), but less perfectly organised and equipped force gathered by Antony in the East. With Actium (31 B.C.) ends the history of naval warfare on a large scale in ancient times.

For the policing of the seas and the protection of the trade-routes, especially those by which the food-supply of Rome travelled, Augustus established a standing fleet. It was not, however, a public and national force, but a service privately organised by the emperor. The crews were at first slaves or freedmen belonging to his household (*familia*). From the time of Claudius non-Roman subjects (*peregrini*) were also enrolled, who received citizenship on their discharge after twenty-six years' service. The squadrons were commanded by *praefecti* of equestrian rank, who had generally earned their promotion by service in the land forces, *e.g.* as *primipili*, legionary *tribunes* or commanders of auxiliary troops.

Of these squadrons (*classes*) the most important were those whose headquarters were at Misenum (on the Bay of Puteoli) and Ravenna (which was connected with the Po by a canal dug in the early years of Augustus's reign). The *classis Misenatium* was responsible for the safety of the western Mediterranean; we find detachments stationed (amongst other places) at Ostia, Forum Julii (Fréjus on the Riviera), Alerion (in Corsica), Caralis (Cagliari in Sardinia), and Panormus (Palermo). To the *classis Ravennatium* belonged not only the Adriatic (with stations at Aquileia, Ancona, Salonae, and Brundisium), but apparently the Aegean also. There was, however, a joint station of both fleets at the Piraeus, as also at Centumcellae, the modern Civita Vecchia, after the building of the new harbour by Trajan.

Other squadrons were the *classis Syriaca* stationed at Seleucia, the harbour of Antioch, the *classis Alexandrina*, which besides protecting the corn-fleet of Alexandria was responsible for the defence of the North African coast (with headquarters at Caesarea (Cherchel) in Mauretania) until Commodus formed a special squadron for that purpose, the *classis Pontica*, taken over by Nero from the client dynasty of the Polemones, which patrolled the Euxine and Propontis, and had stations at Trapezus (Trebizond) and Cyzicus, and the *classis Britannica*, dating from Claudius's conquest of our island (headquarters in Gesoriacum, the modern Boulogne, and stations in the Kentish ports).

The emperors also maintained flotillas on the great rivers. The *classis Germanica*, which patrolled the Rhine and when necessary the North Sea, numbered 1,000 vessels in *A. D.* 16 (see Tac. *Ann.* ii. 6), but many of these were light craft, flat-bottomed barges, &c. The Danube flotilla consisted of two squadrons, the *classis Pannonica* and *classis Moesica*, stationed on the middle and lower Danube respectively. Detachments of the latter are shown on the reliefs of Trajan's Column; and we also see the *classiarii*, clad in a short tunic, employed in roadmaking. Indeed, the *pax Romana* was so firmly established in the waterways that the 'handy men' of the Imperial Navy were regularly employed in peaceful tasks, such as the management of the awnings which protected the spectators in the amphitheatre. The fleets took some part in the civil wars of the Empire, especially that of *A.D.* 69, in which they did good service for Otho and afterwards for Vespasian, who *may* have rewarded the Italian squadrons with the title *praetoria*.

Such in brief outline is the history of the Roman navies. The ships of which they were composed varied greatly in build at different periods. In the Punic Wars the capital ship was the *quinquereme*, which (as Mr. Tarn has said) corresponds with the '74' of Nelson's fleet. In fact, Polybius appears to use the word much as we say 'battleship', and we are not to suppose that the fleets of *quinqueremes* which he mentions consisted solely of vessels which deserved that name. He notes that in the famous inscription of Hannibal in the temple of Hera Lacinia it was stated that in the fleet which he left in Spain in 219 B. C. there were fifty *quinqueremes*, two *quadriremes* and five *triremes*; and we may assume that a percentage of second- and third-rate ships took their place in the Roman squadrons. Probably these were furnished by Rome's allies, while *quinqueremes only* were built by the Romans themselves. (Polybius tells us that a stranded Carthaginian *quinquereme* supplied the Romans with the model of their first battleships in the first Punic War).

We hear of a Carthaginian *hepteres* (warships) at Mylae; on the other hand, some of the Roman allies sent *pentekonters, i.e.* fifty-oared open galleys. The monuments give us no representation of a *quinquereme*; and the question whether such vessels could have had five *superposed* banks of oars has been much debated of recent years. It belongs primarily to the domain of Greek antiquities; for the *trireme*— said to have been invented by Aminocles of Corinth in 704 B. C— furnished the type on which the larger warships were modelled, and its arrangement must first be determined.

163

The explicit statement that its three groups of oars (*'thranite'*, *'zugite'*, and *'thalamite'*) were in fact superposed banks is found in scholiasts and lexicographers, and however small their competence may have been in practical seamanship, they are doubtless drawing upon the stores of Alexandrian learning, which go back to a time when *triremes* &c, were to be seen daily in the harbours of the Greek East. Nevertheless, it has been argued with much ingenuity that ancient warships were built after the fashion of Venetian galleys. These were of two kinds—a *zenzile*, in which the rowers sat in groups of three (all on one level), each pulling one oar, and a *scaloccio*, in which long sweeps were pulled each by several rowers sitting abreast.

To assume that the larger warships of Hellenistic and Roman types were of this latter type no doubt removes many practical difficulties; but it is quite certain, from the evidence of literature and inscriptions, that one man pulled one oar not only in the Athenian *trireme*, but also in the *quadriremes* and *quinqueremes* built at Athens in the fourth century B. C, and it is hard to believe that there was a complete change in the significance of the group of words in Hellenistic times. The galley a *zenzile*, with its oars projecting in sheaves of three from large port-holes, gives us no help; for the word Greek word refers to the three groups of rowers whose names are given above, and if they did not sit in tiers, there can only have been three 'squads' placed astern, amidships and in the bows.

Lastly, the evidence of the monuments (as we shall see) confirms the view that the banks of oars in ancient warships were superposed. It is to be noted that the monster ships built for the Diadochi and more especially for certain of the Ptolemies disappear from ancient warfare in the Roman period, and were doubtless found to be costly and unwieldy failures. The ship of forty banks built for Ptolemy Philopator and minutely described by Callixenus was simply a curiosity, and the same may be said of the vessel of sixteen banks belonging to the Macedonian kings, retained by Philip V at the peace of 197 B.C., but surrendered to Rome in 167 B. C. Livy speaks of it as *'inhabilis prope magnitudinis'* (almost unmanageable size).

But the tendency to reduce the dimensions of warships proceeded yet further. As early as the close of the fourth century B. C. we hear of the names of three Greek crafts, which (if the accepted theory of the Greek warship be true) should mean vessels with one and a half, two, and two and a half banks of oars. How the half-banks (no doubt the upper banks) were placed we do not know; the second (Lat. *biremis*) is represented on monuments of the Roman period. Such craft were largely used by the pirates of the Adriatic and Eastern Mediterranean on account of their superior speed; in fact, the fighting *bireme* used by the Illyrian *corsairs* was called a '*liburnian*'. These vessels formed a large element in the Eastern fleets from the Mithradatic Wars onwards.

Thus, Mithradates Eupator in 88 B.C., besides 300 'decked ships', *i.e. triremes* and higher ratings, had a hundred of the first size Greek ships and one of the second size is mentioned in the following campaign. There were second size ones, too, in the fleet with which Pompey crushed the Cilician pirates. It is commonly said that the civil wars, and especially the Battle of Actium, decided the issue between the *bireme* and the heavier line-of-battle ships in favour of the former, and it is true that the lighter types predominated in the Imperial navy. But this was no doubt because Augustus, having no naval power to fear, was able to discard the expensive types with multiple banks; and it is not clear that his successes in the civil war were gained with *biremes*.

It is hard to say what was the composition of Sextus Pompeius's fleet; Appian notes the fact that his own flagship was a *hexeres* (warship) in such a way as to imply that this was an exception. But the historians are clear on the point that Agrippa outbuilt Sextus Pompeius in the height and weight of his ships, and thus got the better of him at Mylae and Naulochus. Antony determined to outdo him by building yet heavier ships, and several of the one and a half bank ships went into action at the Battle of Actium. The descriptions of the battle show that these were, so to speak, besieged by the lighter vessels of Augustus like floating castles (Appian tells us that after Mylae, 'Sextus Pompeius complained that he had had to fight against "walls, not ships"', thus at Actium the position was reversed); but that the victory was *mainly* achieved by *biremes* is implied by Vegetius only amongst ancient authorities.

★★★★★★

He evidently writes under the influence of the usage, current in his time, by which *Liburna* meant 'warship'; and it is to be noted that he speaks of 'the *Liburni*', *i.e.* the Illyrian contingents, not even of *Liburnae*.

★★★★★★

Floras tells us that Antony's vessels ranged from six up to ten banks of oars, and that the heavier ratings were unwieldy and unserviceable, while the ships of Augustus's fleet ranged from *biremes* to *hexeres*, and this statement may be accepted as correct.

The composition of the Imperial navy may be gathered from the inscriptions found chiefly at Misenum and other places on the Bay of Naples, as well as at Ravenna. Of the names of vessels known to us the greater number are those of *triremes*, and next to these come *Liburnae*, *i.e. biremes*. A few *quadriremes* are known, as well as one *quinquereme* and one *hexeres*. *Liburna*, however, became the conventional name for a warship, and is so used by late writers, even when they speak of the early naval history of Rome. On the other hand, *trierarcha* is the title of a ship's commander, whether his vessel be a *bireme* or a *trireme*. (It is not certain what were the duties of the *nararchus*, who was superior in rank to the *trierarcha*. Mommsen believes that the word means the commander of one of the heavier types of warship).

The scene reproduced on Pl. XLII from the Column of Trajan, which shows the departure of the *classis Ravennatium* from the harbour of Ancona on the outbreak of the second Dacian War in *A. D.* 105, represents both *biremes* and a *trireme*. It would be absurd to draw precise conclusions as to technical detail from a work which, in accordance with the conventions of ancient art, shows just as much as is necessary to tell a contemporary spectator the story which the artist wishes to impart. This is done by selection.

The *praetorian signa* planted in the stern of the lowermost ship show that the guards, and therefore the emperor, are embarked on the fleet (this is clear from the context; otherwise we might suppose that the *classis praetoria* was, as such, entitled to use *praetorian signa*; a *signifer* in the *classis Misenatium* is named in C. I. L. x. 1080); the lantern which hangs from the *aplustre*, or curved stern-post, of the *trireme* in the centre, indicates that the voyage takes place at night (a light was carried at night by the admiral's flagship in ancient fleets); the awning spread over the topmost ship means that it carries the emperor. The arrangement of the oars is evidently determined by the artist's desire to economize detail; but surely it is obvious that superposed banks are represented. The device on the prow of the *trireme*, a sea-monster, points to its name—doubtless the Pistrix, like the vessel of Mnestheus in Vergil. (*Aen.* V. 116).

On a relief from Praeneste in the Vatican, which is probably to be dated to the beginning of the Augustan period, the crocodile takes the place of this monster. It is very possible that this relief, which belonged to a frieze, and was found in the temple of Fortuna, was dedicated in memory of the Battle of Actium; and we see on the prow of the ship one of the towers which, as we know, were in use at that period.

166

(Appian, *B. C.* v. 106, explicitly tells us that Agrippa's ships had towers on both stem and stern, so that there is no reason to question the accuracy of the representation. The stem was, however, the natural place for a single tower). These towers were used as gun-platforms for artillery, and belonged properly to the heavier battleships. The *bireme*, on the other hand, was designed for the ramming tactics inherited from fifth-century Greece, which had for a time given way to the boarding tactics of the earlier Hellenistic period and the Punic Wars. Wall-paintings, now faded, from the Temple of Isis at Pompeii, display a running fight of this type, in which one of the vessels engaged is just sinking. The relief from Trajan's Column shows a single ram; on a frieze in the Capitoline Museum three superposed rams are seen; while ancient writers speak of the ram as of trident shape. One or more upper rams were also used, as on the lowermost ship on Pl. XLII The ram was employed, not merely to charge the enemy's ship, if possible amidships, and sink it, but also to disable it by shooting alongside and carrying away the rudders and oars; it was precisely in manoeuvres of this kind that superiority in speed and training were decisive.

This is clearly emphasized in Appian's account of Agrippa's victory at Mylae; and the advantage of light craft in such a fight was recognized by Philip V of Macedon, who defeated the Rhodians at the Battle of Chios (201 B. C.) by the use of *lembi, i.e.* light piratical ships, generally with a single bank of oars which wrought havoc among the heavy battleships of the enemy when they were no longer able to manoeuvre freely in the *mêlée*. (Livy speaks of Philip's *lembi biremes* in one passage; but this is quite exceptional). Thus the designers of ancient warships were confronted with the same difficulty which besets those of our own time—that of attaining the maximum of strength without undue sacrifice of speed; and the indecisive character of the actual fighting in the last great naval battle of antiquity left the question in reality unsettled, since the victory, due in great part to the flight of Antony and Cleopatra and its disastrous moral effect, deprived the ancient Super-Dreadnought of its *raison d'être*.

Trajan's Embarkation at Ancona (from Cichorius, *Reliefs der Trajanssäule*).

LEONAUR

ALSO FROM LEONAUR
AVAILABLE IN SOFTCOVER OR HARDCOVER WITH DUST JACKET

THE FALL OF THE MOGHUL EMPIRE OF HINDUSTAN *by H. G. Keene—*
By the beginning of the nineteenth century, as British and Indian armies under Lake and Wellesley dominated the scene, a little over half a century of conflict brought the Moghul Empire to its knees.

LADY SALE'S AFGHANISTAN *by Florentia Sale—*An Indomitable Victorian Lady's Account of the Retreat from Kabul During the First Afghan War.

THE CAMPAIGN OF MAGENTA AND SOLFERINO 1859 *by Harold Carmichael Wylly—*The Decisive Conflict for the Unification of Italy.

FRENCH'S CAVALRY CAMPAIGN *by J. G. Maydon—*A Special Correspondent's View of British Army Mounted Troops During the Boer War.

CAVALRY AT WATERLOO *by Sir Evelyn Wood—*British Mounted Troops During the Campaign of 1815.

THE SUBALTERN *by George Robert Gleig—*The Experiences of an Officer of the 85th Light Infantry During the Peninsular War.

NAPOLEON AT BAY, 1814 *by F. Loraine Petre—*The Campaigns to the Fall of the First Empire.

NAPOLEON AND THE CAMPAIGN OF 1806 *by Colonel Vachée—*The Napoleonic Method of Organisation and Command to the Battles of Jena & Auerstädt.

THE COMPLETE ADVENTURES IN THE CONNAUGHT RANGERS *by William Grattan—*The 88th Regiment during the Napoleonic Wars by a Serving Officer.

BUGLER AND OFFICER OF THE RIFLES *by William Green & Harry Smith—*With the 95th (Rifles) during the Peninsular & Waterloo Campaigns of the Napoleonic Wars.

NAPOLEONIC WAR STORIES *by Sir Arthur Quiller-Couch—*Tales of soldiers, spies, battles & sieges from the Peninsular & Waterloo campaigns.

CAPTAIN OF THE 95TH (RIFLES) *by Jonathan Leach—*An officer of Wellington's sharpshooters during the Peninsular, South of France and Waterloo campaigns of the Napoleonic wars.

RIFLEMAN COSTELLO *by Edward Costello—*The adventures of a soldier of the 95th (Rifles) in the Peninsular & Waterloo Campaigns of the Napoleonic wars.

www.ingramcontent.com/pod-product-compliance
Lightning Source LLC
Chambersburg PA
CBHW021107090426
42738CB00006B/545